Some Things Really *Were* Better in the 1950s

?#@*&%!!

Some Things Really *Were* Better in the 1950s

By Lou Johnson

SOME THINGS REALLY WERE BETTER IN THE 1950s © copyright 2011 by Lou Johnson. All rights reserved. No part of this book may be reproduced in any form whatsoever, by photography or xerography or by any other means, by broadcast or transmission, by translation into any kind of language, nor by recording electronically or otherwise, without permission in writing from the author, except by a reviewer, who may quote brief passages in critical articles or reviews.

ISBN: 978-1-59298-367-4

Library of Congress Control Number: 2010940839
Printed in the United States of America
First Printing: 2011
15 14 13 12 11   5 4 3 2 1

Book design by Ryan Scheife, Mayfly Design (www.mayflydesign.net).

BEAVER'S POND
PRESS

Beaver's Pond Press, Inc.
7104 Ohms Lane, Suite 101, Edina, MN 55439-2129
(952) 829-8818 • www.BeaversPondPress.com

To order, visit www.BeaversPondBooks.com
or call (800) 901-3480. Reseller discounts available.

Contents

Foreword *vii*

1. Modern Dress *1*
2. Big Changes from Rock 'n' Roll to Ruination *3*
3. Rock 'n' Roll Results *5*
4. Organized Exercise? *7*
5. Video Games *10*
6. The Draft *13*
7. Kids' Games Turned Into Businesses *16*
8. Family Transportation: Stylish and Functional? *18*
9. Idiot Drivers and the Speed Laws *22*
10. Fashion and Change *24*
11. Older is Better (in Stuff That is) *28*
12. Older But Better in Some Ways *30*
13. The Joy of Computers *33*
14. General Incompetence *35*
15. The Movies *37*
16. Toy Phones? *39*
17. Musical Taste *41*
18. Wonderful Trains and Planes *44*
19. Institutional Rudeness *47*
20. The Death of Print Media *49*
21. E-readers *51*
22. Help? *53*
23. Fat City *55*
24. Offshore *57*
25. God Only Knows *59*
26. Let's Talk About Government…Honesty and Integrity *61*
27. Politically Active Morons *65*

28. Government Incompetence *67*
29. Blue Double Cross *74*
30. Health Care *78*
31. We're Not 9-1-1 for the World *81*
32. Some Things Never Change *85*
33. Work, Workers, Bosses, and Owners *88*
34. Making More Morons *94*
35. Older People Could Use a Little Help *95*
36. Illegal Drugs *98*
37. Punishment Needs Some New Standards *100*
38. The Immigration Problem *102*
39. What We Don't Know Can Hurt Us *104*
40. Guns *107*
41. Israel *110*
42. Blacks *113*
43. Dying *117*
44. Summing Up *120*

Epilogue *124*

About the Author *126*

Foreword

The world today is a pretty sorry place. It and all of its residents could use a little help. Having passed the three score and ten milestone, I'm presumptuous enough to offer a little advice.

I was born in Aberdeen, South Dakota, on July 11, 1936, in a hospital without air-conditioning. The local paper reported the next day that the temperature on July 11 had been 113 degrees—the hottest temperature reported in the United States. The following winter was equally brutal, and of course, the dust bowl was celebrated daily with punishing winds. It had to get better.

Actually, as corny as it may sound, it was a perfect town during my grade school years. We lived in a quiet part of town. I could walk, run, dig foxholes in vacant lots, and ride my bike in the streets with impunity. An occasional bus or car was quickly noted and avoided, but basically the streets belonged to the young. School was close enough for walking. Recess, gym class, and seasonal sports provided for healthy bodies. In those days, it was too early for interest in the opposite sex, so school, sports, and scouting pretty much occupied public time. Reading, radio programs, and family handled the private time.

Just before small-town life began to close in, my father was transferred to Minneapolis. In 1949, the Twin Cities metro area population was about a million—a big city fraught with dangers unknown in Aberdeen. Robbers, perverts, and evil doers of all ilks were easily explained to my mother and me by my father. He had grown up in Chicago. He knew that doors (both on cars and on houses) must be locked, possessions must be carefully husbanded, and strange people should be regarded with caution. Luckily, most of his advice was unnecessary in our quiet, moderately affluent suburb.

Edina, Minnesota's population was about 7,000 when we moved there. And because I arrived the same year as various grade schools entered the town's only junior high school, I wasn't the only stranger. It made the transition easier. Schools were important to our parents. A year later, the community built its first high school. Most of the students intended to go to college so the school had the motives and objectives normally found in private college prep schools. Edina High School was shiny and new and, luckily for us, so was the faculty. They brought a first-job vigor that gave us a world-class education as well as world-class aspirations. Their skills were such that fifty-five years later, I sought my English teacher's counsel and approval for this book.

College choice was daunting. Many of my friends were

accepted by Ivy League schools, and I would have liked to join them, but even with a scholarship, the cost would have been prohibitive for my parents. The University of Minnesota was accessible and affordable and proved to be a wonderful place for personal growth—both intellectual and social. I commuted from home for the first year, and when my father was transferred to Chicago, I moved into my fraternity house.

Living at the Lodge (our name for the house) finished off the last veneer of my only child superiority and made me a better person. I also learned that dust bunnies do not kill, that walking barefoot in the shower does not guarantee athlete's foot, and that many other hygienic truths instilled in me by my mother didn't apply to the real world.

For those of you who view college fraternities with disdain, you should know that far from their elitist reputation, the mix of students was remarkably normal. The cost of living on campus was approximately the same as the dorms for room and board, and my price included weekend parties and the unauthorized kegs of beer. I participated in many campus activities with nonfraternity students and also worked with dance bands most weekends, so my college experiences reflected a cross-section of the campus. And I enjoyed every minute of it.

Since I graduated with a bachelor's degree in humanities, my credentials include my age (seventy-four), a husband (three times), a father (one son, four stepsons), a grandfather (one granddaughter), military service (enlisted man in army reserve), and business experience (banking, sales, booking entertainers, advertising copywriter, and a lifelong musician/bandleader).

During my lifetime, our world has enjoyed better days. Unfortunately, our society has chosen to discard many of the rules I grew up with—actually just about all of the rules I grew up with…except needing someone to love, enjoying good (maybe better-prepared) food, wanting to succeed, and wanting to live long enough to enjoy life. But in most other respects, it's a whole new ball game…and not necessarily a better one. So here are a few of the things that make me sad and mad, and quite a few things that really piss me off.

?#@*&%!!

Chapter 1

Modern Dress

There was a time in the twentieth century when you could tell who was an adult. If you were male, you went from diapers to short pants to long pants. To be a grown-up, you wanted to look like your dad. Dad's dress might vary with his job, but one thing was a constant. When he was dressed up for church, a wedding, or a funeral, and in many business situations, he wore a suit (matching coat and trousers, dress shoes, a white shirt, and a tie). Your mother also followed a set of rules. Church and special occasions required a dress. Sports and other activities also had a set of standards.

Certain clubs and restaurants and employers required a man to be dressed properly. No exceptions. Most schools had dress codes, and private schools required uniforms.

Police officers, firemen, military men and women, and people in many trades were required to wear uniforms while at work...a neat, clean uniform.

Public dress has run amok. Casual Fridays have reached

epic proportions of the unmatched and unkempt with a seasoning of vulgarity to the point that bosses have to push back with rules more appropriate to the regulating of adolescents.

This, of course, is a result of no parenting and no role models.

I blame rock 'n' roll and hippies.

?#@*&%!!

Chapter 2

Big Changes from Rock 'n' Roll to Ruination

Rock 'n' roll did a lot of harm. It was like a cultural bomb. Businessmen lit the fuse when a radio station owner in Omaha invented top 40 radio. Up until the 1950s, radio stations were a positive cultural influence. They felt an unspecified obligation to inform, entertain, and uplift society. Though Federal Communications Commission licensing was more inclined to propriety and honest business dealings, station owners were usually respected members of the community who provided local, world, and national news in addition to music, drama, and commentary designed to better the community.

This programming was expensive, but noble and profitable as well. Almost any reputable old line radio station broadcasted a collection of programs that gave its audience a well-rounded intellectual experience—ranging from sports, live music, news, and network offerings of soap operas, dramas from New York and Hollywood, comedians, the New

York Philharmonic, the Chicago Civic Opera, and the Grand Ole Opry from Nashville. A kid or an adult could become an educated, responsible citizen without changing the dial once. A kid who wanted dance music or jazz had to work to find it.

Then came top 40 radio. Hire five or six announcers to play records and a couple of newsmen to sum up the world in five minutes per hour, and you could go on forever—not to downplay the disc jockeys (as they came to be known). It isn't easy to hold it together for five-hour shifts, but they often weren't the brightest, and their grammatical skills often mimicked lyricists who earned small fortunes with lines like, "He don't love me no more."

The poor English teacher only had an hour a day to undo the barrage of thousands of hours of crap.

Understand that this was not a diabolical plot by an enemy foreign government. This was done by businessmen. Family men, Rotarians, civic leaders, and church goers unleashed this lifestyle-changing movement for profit. Hmmmmmm.

?#@*&%!!

Chapter 3

Rock 'n' Roll Results

It wasn't exactly a revolution in the classic sense, but kids emulated the rock stars' dress codes, eschewed their parents' style of social dancing, and were less concerned with neatness. It was more of a rebellion than a revolution, but the kids simply discarded the structured lifestyle of their parents.

They lived through it, grew up, mated, reproduced, and made a rational decision to rear their offsprings without the structure they endured. In a sense, they became suburban hippies without the grime.

While this might seem like a positive decision on child-rearing in a college dorm room discussion, little free spirits do not always perform in the way that benefits society.

A woman wrote in a newspaper story about a screaming child on an airplane who was so obnoxious that the pilot taxied back to the terminal and put the woman and her child off the plane. What a wonderful thing. Sadly, the airline crumbled under the pressure from the outraged mother, and they bribed the woman with a pay-off that included free tickets and cash. I submit the mother should have been disciplined and perhaps fined for poor parenting.

Planes are a particular horror show if your flight includes a screaming child or a seat kicker, but this is not the only venue for poor parents and their offsprings. They can ruin a restaurant dinner for any number of people on their "one night out," mar a shopping experience, or simply cause outrage at the nuisance caused.

I once watched a kid in a supermarket go the length of a meat counter with a toothpick and puncture nearly every package of meat. God knows how many people were put at risk, and when I mentioned it to the mother, she didn't seem particularly concerned.

My wife has watched unattended children with chocolate covering their hands touching skirts at Target; she has also seen mothers in supermarkets take candy out of self-serve bins and give it to children in shopping carts. With life lessons like these, we should not be surprised by the generation of scofflaws we have created.

Politeness, consideration for others, and routine fair play are history. My wife says that her father could stop her misbehavior with a look. I don't know that he ever enforced the look with corporal punishment, but he probably didn't have to because with proper upbringing, a look was instruction enough.

?#@*&%!!

Chapter 4

Organized Exercise?

Organized sports have not benefitted our kids. When I was growing up (from six to eleven years old), we took care of business ourselves. The big kids or older siblings did the teaching. Life was flexible, and common sense ruled.

If kids were lucky enough to have bikes (they were really scarce during World War II), they didn't want to wreck them, but that didn't stop the kids from riding without holding on the handlebars (it improved your sense of balance). They just didn't do it on crowded streets. And they didn't have helmets either, but experience taught them that banging their heads was not a good thing. Kids also didn't leave their bikes unattended. Bikes, a new Rawlings baseball glove, and other prized possessions required constant diligence.

Older kids groomed the younger ones, trained them, and put them in their place by choosing them last in a pick-up ball game. That made the younger kids work harder and learn faster to gain their approval.

And then when rudimentary organized sports reared its ugly head (in the fourth grade where I lived), we were not the raw stock of youth. We were ready to be honed into jocks. And in those days, baseball was the only organized sport. Nobody in his right mind would have subjected growing, young bodies to the rigors suffered by today's kids.

Now, when kids should be gently exposed to the wonders of the world, they are put in uniforms and forced to groom their undeveloped bodies to conform to the demands of our totally sports-crazy society. The humiliation begins (for boys) when they can't even hit a stationary ball on a rubber pole in a T-ball game. It isn't too bad if nobody can hit the ball, but there is usually a slightly older, bigger, or secretly coached kid who corks one often enough to shame the rest of the kids. The torture doesn't stop with the well-attended games (at least one parent has to drive them to the game). It can be an everyday thing if the coaching dad is particularly zealous about his station or trying to be a winner at this late date.

For the kids this doesn't cripple, it may be a good thing. In this TV/video game/texting/twittering electronic world, physical exercise is dwindling. And in the world of school budget cuts, schools are eliminating physical education for the masses to grant enormous largesse to the organized sports programs. It seems counterproductive for society as a whole to deny the majority of kids their last chance for a healthy lifestyle so the physically fit few can grab trophies or athletic scholarships to college. It would be better for them and society if school prepared students for the regular life they would live when they miss out on an NFL draft.

Kids have been growing up for a long time without needless structures, restrictions, and protections. Kids do benefit from being out in the fresh air, learning from peers, and exercising at their chosen pace. Young jocks will embrace sports, young scientists will study nature, and young readers will sit in the shade and read. And that is as it should be.

?#@*&%!!

Chapter 5

Video Games

What are we doing? In addition to exposing our kids' growing bodies to injuries in the forced exercise of team sports, we are grossly undersupervising our kids' involvement with video "games" popularizing murder and mayhem. Crime novels, violent movies, and crime dramas as TV fodder are a huge part of our culture, but they were created as "entertainment," not as a prep school for cold-blooded killers.

In my youth, the indolent outcasts of my generation were intimately involved with pinball machines, which involved a fair amount of coordination and restraint to score the gazillion points that were rewarded by a free game. The only violence involved an angry bump when the thumbs and forefingers gave way to a little pushing of the machine to encourage the ball's correct descent and resulted in the dreaded "tilt" sign lighting up and the machine itself further disciplining the player by summarily ending the game. And while the player would have happily destroyed the machine, the desire to try again was usually enough to calm the player down. And it only cost another nickel to be humiliated again.

Those were gentler times.

Now, advanced technology allows a kid (in spite of age restrictions requiring an adult purchase) to practice killing soldiers, mafia guys, and police. These are sold as games, but many are so realistic that the military is using similar simulations to train troops while saving on actual ordinance.

What the heck? Kids are kids. Violence has always appealed to them. I played "guns" as a cowboy or Indian. Growing up in the 1940s, we played "war." We had cap guns, wooden "Tommy guns" (if you were lucky enough to have a dad with a jig saw), fox holes, and "victory garden" beets as hand grenades, but we were focused on our country's enemies in Europe and Asia, not the police.

My generation could have handled this new stuff better as well. We read more, played outside more, studied harder, respected authority (even when they were wrong), and generally had a better perspective on adult responsibilities and right and wrong because we were better. And because we had parental guidance, there was no way a kid could have buried himself in a room for hours obsessing on a game.

Remember, in those days, the United States used to lead the world in math abilities and literacy and all of the other good things.

Now our students are ranked 15th in the world, somewhere between the Philippines and Ecuador. The number of dropouts is staggering. Our prisons are overflowing. Kids can't spell (ain't text messaging grand?). They can't make change if the cash register crashes, and now, thanks to the economy, they can't get jobs.

The only good news is for American business. Video games are selling like crazy. The bad news for America is that the military is using similar "games" to train soldiers how to kill people.

?#@*&%!!

Chapter 6

The Draft

Parents aren't what they used to be. I don't know if rock 'n' roll ruined everything, although it's a convenient whipping boy for the mess we're in. It doesn't seem fair to hang everything on music, although it's been blamed at one time or another by somebody going back to Socrates.

Music, hippies, an unpopular war, and woeful political decisions all played their part, but one much maligned institution was discarded, and that was a big mistake. I'm talking about the draft. The draft cleaned up the kids in areas neglected by parents.

I certainly wasn't happy about national service. There wasn't a war. It represented an annoyance, an interruption to the beginning of adult life. I wasn't a draft dodger. I had a college deferment. When I flunked out of school (too many activities, too little studying), I didn't go to Canada or have "too many other priorities," I joined the Army Reserve to limit my active duty to six months instead of the draftees' two years of required service.

I loved it, including basic training. I left the service in the best physical shape of my life. I felt good about the system that was protecting us from the ugly situations in the world. I noticed the flaws, but the overall experience was good. It was also a very important step to maturity. I grew up in a protected white-bread world. No blacks or Hispanics were in any of my schools. My only personal contacts with minorities were with fellow musicians and student leaders in college, and our shared interests eliminated any physical differences.

In my barracks, the other three guys who shared my name and space were black. Fifth Army (geographically Midwestern) drew trainees from Chicago, Detroit, Milwaukee, St. Louis, the Twin Cities, and all the rural areas in between. From street kids to lawyers to farm kids, draftees, reservists, and national guard members made quite an eclectic mix. It was a good experience. When you sleep thirty-six inches away from somebody, you get to know him. You talk about everything…home, family, the army…and you help each other.

Right now, America is too polarized. I don't know if reviving the draft would be a panacea; however, living among strangers whose home situations, intellectual achievements, aspirations, and almost everything else different from yours contributes to your own growth as a person, particularly when your life might depend on the skills and friendship of your bunkmate or the other guy in the foxhole.

The military experience also provided a few benefits our society desperately needs. Discipline! If your parents didn't instill in you a sense of duty, order, and respect for society, the platoon sergeant picked up the gauntlet. Cleanliness! A bald head, the forced cleanliness (required when fifty men sleep thirty-six inches apart), and the fetish for starched, neat uniforms certainly kept things orderly. A healthy lifestyle! Fat guys shed the excess weight. Poor kids ate better food than they had in their homes. And everyone got stronger and tougher and was proud of the changes in his physical condition.

An extra benefit was the rule that you uncover (take your hat off) when you enter a building. It's a rule grown men of all ages should follow, especially the ones who wear baseball caps in restaurants.

?#@*&%!!

Chapter 7

Kids' Games Turned into Businesses

Americans are nutty about sports. That's not necessarily a good thing. School sports are often very dangerous to the players. School sports drain money away from important academic pursuits. And perhaps worst of all, they foster a delusion that sporting skills will lead to a big money job, fan adoration, and a continual sexual circus after the game.

All true; however, in a country of 300 million people, only about ten thousand will earn a living in professional baseball, football, basketball, or hockey. Almost every kid will suffer some kind of injury that will remain a lifelong souvenir of the quest for sports fame and fortune. In my case, it's no cartilage in either ankle. Also, a few will die every year. It reminds you of the Roman Empire, which ended badly.

One of the worst results of tighter money in the school systems is the sacrifice of school bands, drama departments, and physical education programs. Physical education (gym

SOME THINGS REALLY WERE BETTER IN THE 1950s

class) is the only chance the fatties we've raised have to get healthy. But you need sports for school spirit.

Sports doctors have noticed that a body can only absorb so many head bangs before the brain is destroyed.

People have always enjoyed amateur sports. Sixty years ago, kids played baseball, football, and hockey, and then they grew up and went to work. There was no TV. Professional baseball was on the radio. College football games were on the radio. People listened to the games while they did yard work, painted the house, whatever. They didn't squat in front of a TV with beer and snacks every waking moment.

The rest of the world seems to handle it better than we do. Soccer is pretty much the only sport that gets international blood boiling. The fans enjoy banging heads on and off the field. But for most people, team sports are just for kids. Adult physical fitness is accomplished in less lethal surroundings—swimming pools, tennis courts, golf courses, jogging tracks, and walking paths.

?#@*&%!!

Chapter 8

Family Transportation: Stylish and Functional?

When I grew up, one's vehicle indicated one's station. In my small town, the people of substance (who owned or ran everything) drove Buicks or Cadillacs. Then, in descending order were the Chryslers, Oldsmobiles, Mercurys, De Sotos, Fords, Plymouths, and, for a while, Kaisers and Frazers. My dad drove a Mercury company car. While he traveled, my mom and I rode with relatives or took the bus.

For business, people drove trucks. Cars were for fun as well as indicating your place in society, which is why I'm perplexed by the bastardized creations I see now. The most extreme example is the Cadillac truck! No self-respecting aristocrat would drive a Cadillac truck! First of all, most rich people treated their cars with respect. Regular washings and recommended maintenance were a way of life. You didn't fill the trunk with manure because your riches came from a farm; you bought a pick-up for the scut work. If you rou-

SOME THINGS REALLY WERE BETTER IN THE 1950s

tinely hauled three employees around, you bought a truck with a crew cab. You didn't take the family to church with your septic tank repair tools in the open box at the back of your all-purpose vehicle.

The only reason I can think of why these cars are made is so that our young people in the trades can aspire to achieving enough moolah to afford an Escalade.

Then there's the HUMMER! The guy who designed it said (jokingly) that adding a machine gun mount might add some sales, only to shrink back in horror as the GM executives he mentioned it to actually began to discuss the pros and cons of his suggestion.

The auto industry has made its share of bad judgment. One particularly vexing series of mistakes seems to occur when mergers or acquisitions allow them to tamper with an established brand. Ford bought Volvo and screwed it up. The Chinese are attempting to rescue the brand.

When I told a friend the title of this book, he suggested I start immediately on a sequel because there seems to be a never ending list of good old things destroyed.

This one made it in time to be included. I am referring to the demise, at least as of this writing, of another venerable Swedish car, the Saab. The headlines almost universally refer to the Saab as "quirky," implying it attracts an oddball crowd of fans. I confess I am one of them. The cars were "designed to provide transportation under miserable weather conditions." Living in the upper Midwest, a land my ances-

19

tors found to be just as miserable in the winter as Sweden, it seemed an appropriate choice. When the car salesman said, "with snow tires this baby will climb the capitol steps," I had to own it. My Saab was previously owned. The new ones were expensive, but I hoped older tough would be almost as good as new tough. It was.

I was lucky to find a nondealer mechanic who knew and loved European cars. He provided great care for the three used Saabs I owned; however, since GM became involved, he ceased to be the strong advocate of years past. In his judgment, the proud brand had turned into a Saturn with Saab clothes on. Apparently, most of the buyers noticed the difference, too. The question we ought to ask is, "Why?"

Detroit was once the epicenter of new world automotive prowess. In the beginning, the guys who designed and built the cars ran the companies. Then gradually marketing guys took over aided and abetted by cost accountants, and their luck finally ran out. It's too bad for the workers, the community, and America. It's even worse that these dying companies acquired Saab and Volvo and did a number on them. So far there is no buyer for Saab, although I read that a Chinese company is interested in acquiring Saab technology from the pre–General Motors era, so maybe something good will come out of this mess.

It has. Saab has been purchased by a small, high-quality boutique auto manufacturer who promises to restore the brand to its former greatness.

When all is said and done, I guess we can be thankful for one thing, at least GM didn't go after Rolls-Royce. I shudder to think of that magnificent grill tacked onto a Buick frame with a Chevy engine and an "improved" exterior design.

?#@*&%!!

Chapter 9

Idiot Drivers and the Speed Laws

I used to joke with my wife about the drivers in the cars in front of us. A man with a dress hat on indicated an old man driving and required a special watchfulness for erratic driving habits. Now, being an old man who drives, I've found quite a few other danger signs. Most people don't signal their turns. Those who do either have their signals on for a second before they cut you off or wait until they are actually turning to let you know of their intentions. Of course, the major issue is the use of cell phones while driving. Close inspection of almost every weird driver reveals a cell phone in use. The most frightening thing is that almost every huge SUV is piloted by a diminutive woman yakking away, oblivious to the damage her lethal machine can do in a crash. As for those who use hands-free phones, it probably won't affect your driving if you find out you're fired, you lost the order, or your wife is filing for divorce. Don't even mention text messaging.

Of course the speed limits get my special interest. I know there are political reasons for the fifty-five-mile-per-hour limit. I also remember driving on the same primitive two-lane roads when the speed limit was seventy miles per hour. My only gripe is that nobody is arrested for breaking the speed limit. If you're not going to enforce the laws, get rid of 'em. It's really annoying to get the looks when drivers burn by you at eighty in a fifty-five zone. According to the speedometer, my aging Mercedes will go 135 miles per hour. So don't push me too far.

?#@*&%!!

Chapter 10

Fashion and Change

Fashion always seemed like a creation of the devil. In the old days, it just affected women. The new colors, textures, and skirt lengths were important to the women in my family. My mother, aunt, and grandmother (not so much) felt that it was important to be correct and timely in their dress. And that was okay if one could afford it. Their conformity was tempered by small-town good sense. Even sixty years ago, the dictates of New York fashion seemed nutty to normal people. But it is not considered as nutty today.

Men were immune to the infection. While not as regimented as the military, there were standards for men. Businessmen wore dark suits, white shirts, muted ties, and black or dark brown shoes. Police officers, firefighters, postal employees, and many trade people wore uniforms. Construction workers, farmers, and artists wore whatever they wanted.

Now I know that fashion forces retail sales. Drastic changes force more sales. Even the most practical men wouldn't keep wearing Nehru jackets or leisure suits after they were out. However, the male models of my day looked like normal guys. There weren't ads featuring pictures of weight lifters, fat guys, or twiggy boys except maybe in catalogs that catered to their size requirements.

Male models were like the beds in Goldilocks—not too hard, not too soft, just right, normal Paul Newman-type bodies that were in good shape, not grotesquely muscular or thin and ill-looking. The kindest judgment I can make about today's male fashion makers is that they've noticed that a goodly number of editors or ad men appear to be twiggy boys and they know where their bread is buttered. The problem I see is that in our overweight society a lot of guys have arms bigger than the waists on the male models and aren't likely to be customers no matter what the magazines say.

The *New York Times* featured Michael Bastian, who "has hit the magic formula by tailoring classic looks from the '70s and '80s to flatter trimmer (but still human) physiques and egos." I would shout, "Hosanna!" except for the fact that he charges $600 for a pair of frayed cut-off khaki shorts that look exactly like the full-length ones the Army PX sold for three bucks in 1958. The *Times* is right about the physiques, but I'm not quite sure about the egos.

My personal preference is for traditional clothing. And for me glacial changes are the best changes. I recognize others revere the new and different, but I marvel over the incredibly stupid moves that successful businessmen and women are wont to make. Hubris apparently does not guarantee success and probably shuts out remorse as well. "Ya win some, ya lose some." Unfortunately, the rest of us are the true losers.

Banana Republic is a perfect example of a great concept and a successful business—bought, neutered, changed, and degraded into the ordinary. Beloved by fans everywhere, the original store gave one access to the clothing and accouterments of adventurers, soldiers of fortune, and explorers. It's nearly impossible to quantify the panache one feels racing to catch a plane with a "foreign correspondent's bag" swinging on your shoulder. Now Banana Republic looks like "Welcome to college week at Macy's." To find the original stock, you have to go to an outfitter in Nairobi or military supply store in Rawalpindi.

Then there's the ignorance of the young hotshot manager who takes an established brand that has exuded quality for over a hundred years and "freshens" the appeal. Burberry, for anyone under thirty, is best represented by the trench coat, designed in 1914 to keep British Officers warm and dry during the brutal days and nights of trench warfare. For nearly one hundred years, it has been the ne plus ultra of rainwear. The "updated" trench looks pretty much the same on top. The problem with the new and improved version is that it barely covers your ass—not exactly practical as rainwear. And people capable of plopping down $2,195 for a raincoat might just expect it to protect the trousers of their $6,000 suit.

Unfortunately, there may be enough affluent fashion-crazed idiots to save the manager's job, but when they rush to embrace the next Nehru jacket, the traditional customer will gravitate to a new traditional vendor and probably won't return, nor should they.

?#@*&%!!

Chapter 11

Older is Better (in Stuff, That is)

We (the mature folks) are pretty sure about that, but it's nice when a forty-year-old "kid" editor discovers it. A snooty magazine I get reports that luxury items have been so debased of late that old-line aristocratic snooty people are now seeking out one-of-a-kind purchases that the hedge fund arrivistes or their wives won't be able to find or appreciate without half a lifetime's preparation. It all boils down to the ability to recognize quality when you see it.

It needn't be expensive either. Stanley Marcus in cataloging the best of darn near everything included Sara Lee pound cake as a winner in the dessert category—not the most expensive, just the best. And the new snooty magazine's listing of $3,000 shoes and ungodly expensive gold baubles also mentioned flannel sheets from L. L. Bean that are winning the affection of the 500- to 1,000-thread-count crowd.

If you choose wisely and really like what you buy, it's especially sweet to see your personal choices skyrocket in value when the rest of the world catches up. I think the long-term rich folks have an advantage over the rest of us. Their families teach them to buy good stuff that retains its value and use it and love it as long as it hangs together. They always look great. Their houses are comfortably worn, and that's okay.

Not convinced yet? The *New York Times* is recommending thrift shops, mainly because the older stuff is of much higher quality than the new stuff in expensive stores.

?#@*&%!!

Chapter 12

Older But Better in Some Ways

A famous author said goodbye to an old Olivetti Lettera 32 portable typewriter that he had bought (used) from a pawnshop in the early '60s. Guessing that he had written over five million words on the machine that had never needed repairs, he reluctantly parted with it when it gradually died of old age. Such was his love for the instrument that he searched and found a "practically new" replacement on eBay. He paid $11 plus $19.95 for shipping.

I also had one of these beautiful machines. Touted for its lightness (aluminum frame), beauty (won design prizes when introduced), and popularity with foreign correspondents (that's what finalized my purchase), I finally parted with mine as word processing became a required skill, particularly helpful with the constant nitpicking changes inflicted on a freelance ad writer. My Lettera wasn't perfect (for me anyway). A strong touch often caused it to skip, and a too soft touch didn't always print, but it was beautiful and very portable,

SOME THINGS REALLY WERE BETTER IN THE 1950s

and even though I never became a foreign correspondent, I basked in the aura of what might have been.

My introduction to computers involved an Apple 2E. As a copywriter for a couple of major electronics retailers, I wrote thousands of ads promoting computers, often implying that a computer purchase would guarantee your child's future success in life or at least admission to a prestigious college. And I believed it. My writing capabilities increased exponentially. I could write quickly, correct mistakes without using white out, move words and whole paragraphs, and doctor the copy quickly at the creative director's whim. It was slick. I graduated to a Mac that was even slicker and quicker. WOW!

While I was creating, my colleagues (who were twenty years younger) were playing games, trading screensavers, and plenty more. I'm not sure we had access to the Internet, but every other trick in the book was tried and passed around. I, on the other hand, simply wrote, revised, printed, and saved my work. No fooling around or kid's games for me. Consequently, I am one of the computer ignorant types who curse the pointy-headed geniuses who have refined computers to be so helpful that I am constantly weighing whether I should throw my computer out the window or take a hammer and deal with it in the privacy of my den.

Now, writing, printing, and saving my work provide constant challenges. The word-processing program exerts constant pressure correcting spelling before a word is complete, forcing punctuation that's not wanted, and dictating where and how to save my work. It stifles any attempt at cleverness, and with four writing programs available, it won't even allow me to save my work if I triggered a different program by accident. Recently when I asked it for help, it seized up (stopped and remained unchanged through nearly a half hour of my pleading fingers). In a fury, I turned the computer off only to be chided when I turned it back on that I had not properly exited and confronted me with another fight.

Two other infuriating characteristics are the hypersensitivity of the keyboard, brushing a key or even breathing on a key is enough to launch a commercial or a program "conveniently" located near (or below the arrow used to scroll). And the brilliantly designed keyboard allows a fat-fingered touch typist to destroy an hour's work by missing the shift key and landing on the control key. Only a pointy-headed engineer using two fingers to type could have come up with this design and left it uncorrected for twenty years.

I'm sure my problem is exacerbated by my distaste for studying manuals that certainly would increase my computer fluency, but this illustrates a need that has existed since day one. I believe the general public (especially the older general public) would like using a computer to be as simple as driving a car. I want to turn on the key and go. I don't want to calculate whether the oil pressure and temperature are appropriate for today's drive or how to rebuild the engine, which brings me back to the Olivetti Lettera typewriter. It filled a need, it always worked, it was beautiful, and it made me feel like a foreign correspondent.

?#@*&%!!

Chapter 13

The Joy of Computers

I have just planned, and I hope successfully executed, a weeklong trip to Arizona. I called my frequent flier program's phone number. After a twelve-minute wait (my phone has a timer), I spoke with someone, made reservations for my wife and me, got a confirmation number, and asked for a confirmation e-mail. It arrived with incomplete information and no mention of my wife's name or ticket. A second call (with another twelve-minute wait) got me to India and another e-mail acknowledging my wife and the fee for her ticket, but still incomplete information.

   I called two hotels (in different cities), made reservations, and got an undecipherable (for me) e-mail attachment apparently confirming my reservation from the first hotel. The other hotel sent a perfectly readable confirmation. One out of two ain't bad. But I still needed another call to the airline to discuss a couple of details, like whether there were meals on the flight.

I understand I am computer illiterate. However, I am a computer illiterate customer! Planning how to spend a considerable amount of money should not be an ordeal. What would have been easily accomplished with a conversation in 1970 is now muddied by "helpful" technology—not a good thing.

I have read that certain companies are intending to charge for mailed statements. They intend to offer e-mail statements gratis. I take this to mean that some 30-year-old bean counter has decided to save money by attempting to convert to a paperless operation. Good for him, not so good for the computerless customers. The business part of my brain recognizes the reason for this, but the outraged elder part thinks the idea stinks. I could fall back on the old (really old) idea that the customer is always right (a wonderful, but forgotten concept). My new idea is a genuine concern that personal financial security is rushing off a cliff. If hackers can break into the Pentagon's supposedly secure Web site, I fear for all of the financial information in basic business transactions left in the care of thirty-year-old bean counters.

?#@*&%!!

Chapter 14

General Incompetence

I had a friend who owned some women's clothing stores. He didn't pay much for young women with some college experience to work at the store (the thrill of the fashion business was a powerful lure), but often he didn't get much for his money. I remember his saying that if the cash register failed to function, the workers couldn't make change. Subtracting $16.75 from $20 isn't space-age math, but they couldn't do it. I understand fast-food giants have pictures of the burgers on the cash registers. I don't understand how today's workforce holds jobs.

My wife went to pick up her medical records. After being ignored until the girl at the counter finished describing last night's date to a co-worker, the girl checked under the counter and handed my wife a manila envelope. While waiting for an elevator, my wife noticed "2 of 2" written on the envelope and went back to the office where the same vacant girl looked and found the matching "1 of 2" and handed it to my wife, thus sparing my wife another twenty-mile drive to fetch it.

Medical offices seem to be uncommonly lucky at finding and keeping incompetents. That's the only explanation for unmade or improper appointments, failure to transfer records or X-rays to other physicians, abrupt communications with troubled and often elderly patients, capped off by a particularly sensitive cancer doctor who actually has a sign on the wall reading, "If you wish to talk with me for more than fifteen minutes, make another appointment."

I find it hard to fathom how these people get and hold jobs. But in 2010, with 10% of the workforce unemployed, we should be able to do better than this. And I don't mean by looking overseas for workers.

?#@*&%!!

Chapter 15

The Movies

I'm almost embarrassed that it took me this long to address a crucial lack in today's entertainment scene. Movies have ceased to require stories. Films are no longer built upon the foundation of cohesive scripts. I have the feeling that the legendary perfect pitch that would fit on a matchbook has been superseded by six words: killings, explosions, car chases, nude scenes. Not every movie in my youth included a world-class story, but many did. Often management's cheapness dictated the use of classic stories whose copyrights had expired (no author to pay). The plus to the public was that these were great stories and they became great movies, usually suitable for all ages.

Today, unfortunately, movies reflect the vulgarity and dangers of life without any mellowing of the experience that was a part of most great books and plays. Reduced attention spans dictate quick cuts, minimum dialog (easily translated for the overseas markets), and lots of gunfights, explosions, and combat (every culture is familiar with the horrors of war). And God forbid any lengthy periods of dialog—they're making movies, not teaching a philosophy class. Gone is right triumphing in the end. Gone is sensitivity, preparation for adult life, morals, and codes of conduct. The movie business is laying it out there for the lowest common denominator. Room temperature IQs will have no trouble being amused. There are more of them now, and most of them can still afford a ticket.

I find that about the only place to watch a good movie today is on Turner Classic Movies on cable television. Many people my age share my opinion. We all feel that Ted Turner's largess is providing about the only outlet for the truly wonderful movies from the past. My fear is that the young people running everything on television today will replace the channel with "Bad Marriages in Suburbia" or "Survival in a Medium-Security Prison."

?#@*&%!!

Chapter 16

Toy Phones?

When I was a kid, the lure of a toy phone was fleeting. They were brightly colored, looked like smaller versions of real phones, and had ringers you cranked, and that was it. The thrill was gone in a few minutes unless your fertile mind enabled you to carry on one-sided conversations designed to be overheard, but any kid that smart usually scuttled the phone and registered his or her demands directly.

Now, as you already may have surmised, my use of "toy phones" is a term of derision. Understand first, I have a history of appreciation of gadgets, especially small gadgets. I had one of the first transistor radios in America. Dinky flashlights, calculators, and the entire stock of the dearly departed Sharper Image make the hair on my neck stand up. However, I am reaching my limit.

I once had a young boss, who had one of the first cellular phones, back when you needed a sidecar for the battery. His job was his life. His importance was unbounded. Most of us relished the chance to escape his clutches while in a car on the way to a meeting, at home on a weekend, a wilderness tour, etc. I'm glad I'm retired. With cell phones, wireless Internet, and God forbid all usable on a plane, I don't think I could grit my teeth long enough to hold a job. But that's just the preamble.

I'm old, but still capable of recognizing progress. When cell phones fit easily into a pocket or purse, that made sense (now that I'm retired). When e-mail became accessible, that made sense. Take pictures, okay. Watch movies…why in God's name would anyone want to watch movies on a phone? Take your pulse, okay. Listen to music, okay. But 35,000 games? Is everybody under seventy crazy? Do you all want to spend the rest of your life in a mental cave? Even if the cave were portable, always ready to serve up the stuff you already knew and enjoyed? In the dark?

I don't see civilization ending if a high school dropout can earn big bucks creating a crazy (to me) app. However, if the rest of society simply "auditions" the 35,000 apps, it seems like it may slow business, family life, and general socialization of the human race a little too much for my taste. I'm afraid the whole concept reminds me of a pacifier. The baby sucks on it, and even if no milk comes, it's comforting. The baby then grows up. I'm not sure the analogy holds up when I substitute the new technological breakthroughs.

?#@*&%!!

Chapter 17

Musical Taste

I am a musician. I started a dance band in 1953. The music we learned and played was the dance music our parents enjoyed. It included a variety of musical styles: swing, Dixieland, show tunes, ballads, big band hits, and the popular music of the period. We tried to duplicate the popular sounds of the day (as much as you can with a five-piece combo). We optimistically tried to give a jazz flavor to the music. People liked it. They paid us to play for them.

In those dark ages, some natural ability and a good deal of practice were required to please our public. For over fifty years, music has been a profitable avocation and a wonderful experience for me. It has given me great pleasure, my closest friends, and a lifetime of incredible memories.

It's hard to explain the musical scene in 1953 to almost everyone under seventy. Making records was a technically difficult process. As a result, there were only about a half dozen cities in America that had record companies. They had total control over the musicians and singers who made records and insisted on high-quality talent, and they also dictated what was to be recorded. This wasn't all bad because the talent they selected was really talented, and the music was of high quality and often had been made popular by touring bands and artists. They created the desire for the records, which almost guaranteed success and a lot of great music.

That all changed in the mid-1950s. Tape recordings eliminated the complicated machinery needed to produce records. Now anybody could record a song, get it produced, and sell it. Vocal ability, voice training, and professional skills were no longer necessary. A guitar, four chords, and a drummer made music. And kids loved it. No matter how primitive, simple, and basic it seemed to us, kids loved it. Anybody (creative) could be a star. In the old days, you had to be a trained singer. Now, every kid who got a guitar and a sound system for Christmas was sure he was going to be Elvis or Buddy Holly. Music got down and dirty, said what the kids were thinking, and gave them a beat to dance to.

We, the more mature, professional, jazz-oriented musicians, still had business from older people, formal dances, wedding receptions, and charity balls catering to the adult crowd. We survived by filling a need. We pleased our customers by playing appropriate music for each situation, including quiet background music when required. I don't have to explain this to anyone who has been at a wedding reception that featured a rock band.

SOME THINGS REALLY WERE BETTER IN THE 1950s

I really don't mean to patronize rock music. It has produced many beautiful, spirited, and complicated records that will stand the test of time, probably better than the bodies of older dancers as their gyrations tax their old muscles and knees.

I'm afraid that like the old soldier in the poem, I and my musician friends will slowly fade away, although it's interesting to imagine the fortieth reunion parties of the class of 2009 trying to do something on the dance floor to relive the rap hits of today.

?#@*&%!!

Chapter 18

Wonderful Trains and Planes

The old days were a lot better for travelers. I grew up in a small town in South Dakota. In 1944, eight transcontinental trains stopped in my hometown every day. Though remote in many senses, the town was truly connected to the entire world. A coach passenger (in the least expensive seat) could read, nap, enjoy a meal, have a drink, and arrive in downtown Minneapolis refreshed and ready to work, shop, or party.

Today, there are no train service, no bus service, and only a few puddle-hopping passenger flights to Minneapolis a day. Perhaps a north–south flight option, but otherwise it's a mind-numbing five-and-a-half-hour drive at the speed limit with minimum comfort stops.

The railroads were given alternate sections of land all across the country to build these railroads. Let's see what they got—3,000 square miles of land, one mile on the north side of the railroad the next mile on the south side of the tracks all across the country, and a total amount of 1,920,000 acres of free

SOME THINGS REALLY WERE BETTER IN THE 1950s

land to connect the country. They got it, cashed in, and then decided about ninety years later that passenger service was too expensive and simply shut down the principle method the country's population had to move about the country.

You can say that the nationwide freeway system caused the problem, but Europe has high-speed freeways and still manages to have the best rail systems in the world. I'm afraid good old corporate greed is the cause, and it didn't end with the railroads.

The old days in the air were better, too. Until the railroads shut down, air travel was for the rich, the busy business people, and the people who had to travel thousands of miles in a short time. And it was glorious. The least expensive ticket provided large, comfortable seats (in coach), real meals with real plates and silverware, and pleasant, attentive service. One could only imagine the indulgences possible in first class—champagne for sure. Federal government price regulations guaranteed the same ticket prices on all of the routes so service and food quality really determined one's choice of airline. The tickets were also interchangeable so if you wanted to travel before your scheduled flight and there was space available on a competitive airline, you simply handed the attendant your ticket and were on your way.

That was then. Now even if we accept the indignities of the security checks, air travel is almost universally despised. Insane charges for every nitpicking possibility have been the final straw. The owner of the leading low-cost airline in

Europe has proposed charging to use the bathrooms. I have the feeling that a plane loaded with drunk soccer fans would probably successfully challenge that idea (or render the plane unusable until the seats were dried and deodorized).

The particularly sad element in this story is that many of the airlines were intelligently managed until they were crippled in leveraged buyouts by greedy hustlers who stripped them of everything of value and left them especially vulnerable to high fuel prices and the recession.

?#@*&%!!

Chapter 19

Institutional Rudeness

"Dear William,

I know you're the kind of man who's open to new investment opportunities...."

This is not the way I want to be introduced to someone who's pitching a means of spending my money. I understand these marketing techniques. I spent a copywriter's nightmare year working for one of the largest direct mail sales organizations in the country. I'm simply against the presumption of intimacy implied by using a person's first name. There may be a place for a folksy approach somewhere, but not when you're asking strangers for money. "Dear Mr. Lovejoy" or "Dear Ms. Robinson" would cover everyone in business presentation.

Then, of course, there is the business phone answered by a machine. What a nice beginning or continuation of a business relationship. You're interrogated by a machine so the wrong clerks won't be troubled by a customer's question they can't answer. Finally, when the machine infuriates you to the bursting point, you are transferred to limbo. In the old days, limbo was silent, but now to make sure you know you're still connected, you're treated to music. While that isn't necessarily a bad thing, someone figured you may still need encouragement to keep holding, so now the music is interrupted, sometimes as often as every fifteen seconds, to tell you how important your call is to the business and that the one person taking care of the entire country is busy helping other customers in the order of their calls. One nice thing about some phones is that they have built-in timers for your calls. I once waited twenty-five minutes for the telephone company's repair service to answer.

Too often, if you're really unlucky, your plea for help gets shunted to India or the Philippines, which, while helpful to the bottom line, plunges customer relations to the absolute nadir.

?#@*&%!!

Chapter 20

The Death of Print Media

A lament about lost treasures would be incomplete without reporting the sadness I feel about the shrinking world of newspapers and magazines. And I mean shrinking in a couple of different ways. Newspapers have diminished in size slowly and uniformly. I don't think an antitrust committee is required, but the three papers I read (the *Minneapolis Star Tribune*, *Wall Street Journal*, and *New York Times*) are all significantly smaller in page size than they were a year ago. In addition, the recession has greatly reduced the thickness of the papers (with the exception of the last ditch stand of advertisers during the holiday selling period), and I suspect a good deal of advertising will never return. And magazines that used to require a derrick to move a small pile of them can now be blown away by a light breeze.

Perhaps the public's reaction is, "Who cares?" In a world where updated news hits the Internet almost immediately, followed by the TV and radio news stations, a case can be made that the loss of print media doesn't indicate a tightened control on information. That's true, of course, if we just want the facts; however, it's the in-depth reporting and analysis that separates the thinking public from the twits. I mean no derision. I am referring to the two-finger communicators who seem to inform everybody about everything that can be communicated in 140 words or less. Actually, I do mean derision. Another unattributed quotation says it all. "Tripe, at the speed of light, is still tripe."

It may not even matter in the near future if we don't do something about the current educational systems. Substantial numbers of children don't graduate from high school, and only about a quarter of the graduates are equipped to attend college. For those who do make it to college, it seems likely they'll read *War and Peace* on cell phones, allowing for multiple rechargings of the device. But while these pocket devices that do everything are amazing, it's frightening to contemplate the effects of a catastrophic worldwide loss of electric power on a Kindle and iPhone society. Pfffft! There goes all of the recorded history in the world.

For those of you who do care about the printed word: subscribe, give gifts, thank the advertisers, and pray.

?#@*&%!!

Chapter 21

E-readers

E-books are just the thing we need to advance society. Now I'm not against gadgets per se. I was among the first to buy a transistor radio. I understand the need to be first, to be different, although as the song from Chorus Line says, "different ain't good" or something to that effect. Some of my contemporaries wax enthusiastically about their Kindles. It takes all kinds.

I'm sure e-books are here to stay. But not for me. And not because I'm not a reader. I subscribe to three daily newspapers and fifteen or twenty magazines and actually peruse all junk mail. I have a Barnes & Noble discount card and make frequent use of my local library, but I can't see a need to pop $350 for an e-reader.

First, I like to read in a bathtub. And I don't know what I'd do if I dropped the e-reader on the floor and ruined it. I don't know how people expect to scroll over each page of an electronic newspaper or magazine. I don't how you can clip out an article or copy it. I don't know how you can fold down the edge of a page to return to a great thought or even mark the page just before you fall asleep.

These are the logical reasons for me to remain in the past. An equally logical reason, and possibly the most compelling one, is the cost of the reading material. Many if not most of my books come from garage sales, estate sales, and used paperback traders. If I drop them in the bathtub, leave them on planes, or spill coffee on them, I'm out a quarter or fifty cents. Beautiful new books from the library are free. And that leaves me with enough cash to patronize Barnes & Noble when I have to have a book immediately.

With an e-book, the price of immediacy and cachet of the Kindle is cash on the barrel for each book right now. And when you want to loan a treasure to your best friend, can you e-mail it or hand over whatever the e-book people gave or sent to you? Are you violating copyright laws? Can they catch you violating copyright laws? And how long before your e-reader gets a little worn looking, and what happens when it dies? Do the books perish with the machine?

And last but not least, what are you using to fill in the space the books used to occupy on the shelves of your library?

?#@*&%!!

Chapter 22

Help?

Help! If we get any more "help" from the businesses who sell us things or services, there is going to be an insurrection. If you're old enough, you can remember when every store had people stationed in every department to actually help you make your selection. Any business dependent on phone service had banks of operators instantly available to serve you. Now they save a lot of money. Instead of actually hiring people to help you, they make recordings that repeat over and over again how anxious they are to help you while you wait and wait and wait for someone in a foreign country to be unequal to the task.

I have nothing against the developing world. But with nearly 10% of our neighbors out of work in the United States, I think it's reasonable to keep these jobs in America and hire people who are familiar with American speech and thought processes...people who can actually do the job. And it isn't just service industries.

It saddens me to remember World War II. We were able to build a Liberty ship (that's a huge ocean-going ship capable of carrying troops, trucks, tanks, and everything else to a war across the sea) every day, convert our auto plants to make tanks, and marshal disparate industries into production teams to supply anything we needed to win the war. Recently, the army had to buy black berets from the Chinese.

One by one our "essential" industries have been dumped in favor of cheaper suppliers elsewhere. This may be good business, but it is not good for America. HELP!

?#@*&%!!

Chapter 23

Fat City

America is too fat. The editor of *Vogue* describes Minnesotans as "little houses." A Congressman decides the poor aren't really poor because they're fat. Many blame the fast-food industry for pushing inexpensive, greasy, often delicious, unhealthy food. As a member of the clean-plate club, inspired by parents who frequently spoke at dinner of the starving Chinese during World War II, I carry more body weight than the health gurus recommend. So, what to do?

First of all, almost everyone who reads or watches *Oprah* knows that lean and mean is a better lifestyle. Well, maybe not mean. Ignorance is no excuse…and hardly possible. What's wrong with us? Oh I suppose cars, fast food, TV, video games, sedentary lifestyles, suburban living, and stupidity all play a part.

There is a point, however, when anyone with a brain should pause and reflect on his or her girth. Let's recognize that at 300 pounds, people who are not sumo wrestlers or

NFL linemen should button their lips, get up off of their asses, and make a few changes in their diets and lifestyles.

With my having watched Oprah's guests, mommies don't seem to be part of the solution. I don't know what the answer is, perhaps jail time for a parent who keeps delivering burgers and french fries to a bedridden 400-pound lump of a child would be a starting point. Why should the public have to pay for a platoon of paramedics to pry them out of their beds and cart them off to hospitals while they are weaned off of their destructive habits?

Just as an aside, with airlines opting for seventeen-inch-wide seats, why should a "normal" body have to be stuffed into a coach seat with a grossly overweight companion whose body overflows into every space above and below the arm rest? Some airlines are requiring passengers "of size" to buy an extra seat when they fly. Okay with me. And by the way, per an article in the June 9, 2009, *Wall Street Journal*, "the Air Carriers Access Act, which requires airlines to accommodate disabled and physically impaired passengers doesn't cover obesity." Everybody seems to be on the same page. Again quoting the article, "'We're willing to pay for what we are rightfully using,' says Peggy Howell, spokeswoman for the National Association to Advance Fat Acceptance." On behalf of a grateful public, I say, thanks!

?#@*&%!!

Chapter 24

Offshore

Offshore. It has a nice ring to it. It suggests leisure, warm water, gentle surf, sandy beaches. Unfortunately, it really means crooks, lost jobs, and evil promulgated by out-of-control assholes.

First of all, crooks love the opportunities presented by offshore enterprises. Certain cultures accept the bribe more readily than others. Certain emerging nations are not equipped to understand complicated financial entities and deal with them. Certain leaders are concerned only with enriching themselves. Many do not respect the extradition treaties more mature governments expect from a functioning nation. One thing is certain: the bad people know how to exploit a situation like this. And that's bad enough.

Then there are rich people who believe that taxes are an outrage, feel justified in cheating their government by using numbered bank accounts, hiding taxable profits, and using all forms of subterfuge to escape their obligations. That's almost worse because they don't have to cheat to survive.

Then there's the corporation that shifts its manufacturing to plants in Mexico, China, India, and emerging nations with low wages and no environmental protections for the workers or the community from toxic manufacturing processes or toxic waste contamination of the community at large.

America seems to be drifting from active Christianity, but not enough to overlook the scriptures, particularly the Ten Commandments. I suppose the corporate lawyers could argue that "Thou shall not kill" means one is prohibited from shooting or stabbing the victim, but that the commandment does not directly forbid killing one slowly and horribly with toxic poisons in the manufacturing process.

You may recall that businessmen shipped toxic children's pajamas that were prohibited from being sold in the United States to Africa to be sold in a more permissive country.

?#@*&%!!

Chapter 25

God Only Knows

Up until now, I've tried to deal with lost pleasures that, while wonderful, are more nostalgic memories than critical losses to the future of America, dear departed niceties rather than critical societal issues. Now come the important stuff.

I am troubled when I hear America is a religious country. At one point, people called it a Christian country although I understand that Jews arrived in Baltimore shortly after the Pilgrims made their famous landing. I suppose Christians would still qualify as the largest religious community. There are many versions of Christianity, and the Roman Catholics would probably be the largest sect. From then on, it moves into various other Christian groups, Jews and other splinters of religious practice, Mormons, Muslims, Hindus, Buddhists, and so on. Most of them have a version of the Golden Rule in their creeds, and with a few exceptions, killing people is not acceptable and charity is desirable. Most members of

Congress profess to being believers and openly practice their respective faiths on the day they spend in worship.

Then how do you explain what happens in Congress from Monday through Friday? "Thou shall not kill" doesn't affect voting for wars or the death penalty, although fetuses the size of an eye drop merit protection. And nobody considers "What would Jesus do?" when voting to stop giving school breakfasts to poor children. And I don't believe Jesus said, "comfort the sick only if you can balance the budget." It used to be harder for a rich man to get into heaven than putting a straw through a needle, but Goldman-Sachs is just too big to fail. What the heck, those people out of work and their homes probably can't make a political contribution anyway. People are starving and living in cars (if they're lucky), and Congress continues to drop huge earmarks on everybody who contributes to their election campaigns.

We've probably got the government we deserve. Most of the voters seem to go for the candidate who is against gay marriage or for machine guns on sale everywhere, against abortion and sex education and for teaching the Biblical version of creation and against teaching evolution. And the sickest thing about all of this is that most of these voters would swear that they believe in God and love America and Americans—just not the "lazy" jobless, homeless people who expect everything to be handed to them on a silver platter.

?#@*&%!!

Chapter 26

Let's Talk About Government... Honesty and Integrity

In the 1960s as a salesman for 3M, I called on a large sign shop in Washington, D.C. After many years in business, the owner said he would only take orders from the Republican or Democratic national committees. In some painful experiences with senators and congressmen, he never got paid for his work (making lawn signs, bumper stickers, etc.). Regardless of the party, if the candidate lost the election, the committee placing the order never paid the bill. The committee disbanded and closed the office, and there was no one to dun or sue. When the candidates won, their handlers never paid the bills either. And in one case, when the owner pressured for payment, his business was examined by the Department of Labor who discovered his employee time clock was a few minutes off. He was forced to pay additional wages to everyone he had employed for the past three years. From then on, he would only work for national committees because there was someone to sue after the election.

On a totally different note, my band played several jobs for a national presidential candidate, including an election-night party. Having met some of the candidate's handlers on earlier jobs, we were talking with them as we set up for the evening. One of them said that they almost didn't have the necessary scaffolding for the TV crews and press. Apparently the vice presidential candidate had come to town several months earlier, ordered scaffolding for a press conference, and skipped town without paying the bill. Therefore, the company said it would provide scaffolding only if it was paid in cash for both jobs before they set up the equipment.

There are apparently good reasons that TV and radio stations require cash with copy on all political ads.

Politicians seem to have a more businesslike arrangement with lobbyists…if they want an ongoing relationship.

Politicians are the price we pay for democracy. According to some wag, Congress delivers the equivalent of movie stardom to ugly, verbose, pushy, and possibly criminal people. It must provide good value to these folks because they spend millions of dollars to acquire a relatively modest (their definition) salary and then constantly raise even more money to hold on to the job year after year.

Unfortunately, most of the money they raise comes from businesses or groups that stand to profit from a sympathetic ear and a friendly bias (engendered by the amount of campaign cash they provide). Needless to say, their wishes do not often coincide with those of the public at large.

And if that isn't bad enough, the interminable obfuscating debates are boring at best and so time consuming that a motion to cut the grass at national monuments can take weeks while really important legislation like universal health care languishes.

In a TV commercial in 2009, Congress is peopled by firemen. They listened to the proposal by the chairman. They quickly (as their job requires) assessed the situation. And they voted by acclimation and left. What a novel idea—no interminable hearings and no running at the mouth—simply understanding the proposal and voting on it. If you doubt my assessment, check out C-Span. After a couple of hours with C-Span, watching paint dry will seem like the last two minutes of the Super Bowl.

Why are we wasting our money on the Congress we have?

William F. Buckley once said something like "I would rather be governed by the first 535 people in the Boston phone book." Hubert Humphrey recognized "the trouble with representative government is that it's representative." Unfortunately, today it's peopled with narrow-minded ideologues, nut cases, and criminally involved minions of lobbyists. It ain't 1776, folks. Even the thoughtful statesmen of my youth are historical characters, and the country shows it.

As of this writing, while our country is involved in two wars, a crashed economy, 10% unemployment, and millions of people losing their homes, Congress is debating the lack of treatment of concussions by professional football teams, whether gays should be allowed to marry, and whether to apply billions of dollars to rebuild Iraq and Afghanistan while questioning the need to care for our citizens, rebuild our crumbling country, or even provide proper care for our wounded soldiers because of our burgeoning national debt.

Gone are the days of a collegial governing. Gone is the recognition that differences in politics are subordinate to the general well being of the country. What's left is a sorry world where the exact words provided by health-care lobbyists are read into the congressional debates by congressmen masquerading as their independent thoughts. It's amazing what spending $609,000 per day on lobbyists for six months can do to influence legislation.

Reading a daily newspaper gives one a clue as to why anyone would spend millions of dollars to be elected to a job that pays a couple of hundred thousand dollars a year. It's a very good living.

?#@*&%!!

Chapter 27

Politically Active Morons

The Texas School Board has a near majority of "Christian" morons. They are trying to dictate that the Biblical version of creation is given equal weight with the teaching of evolution in the Texas public schools. If the "Christians" truly represent a near majority of voters in the state, they can have a severely deleterious effect on American education. Major textbook publishers revise their products to match the Texas requirements. (With Texas being one of the largest bulk customers, might makes right.) A recent effect of the moron majority is reflected in the former president's protection of the right to life of discarded stem cells until they reach the garbage can.

I suppose Texas majority rule will someday affect the scientific knowledge of America's high school students; however, American universities should refuse to admit students from any state that uses the sullied textbooks to any medical or technical school that requires a scientific education.

Recently, the pope said that the use of condoms does not prevent HIV or AIDS. This is another case of a Christian moron whose revealed knowledge is counter to worldwide scientific information.

It seems appropriate to quote a learned Roman Catholic about now. Senator Daniel Patrick Moynihan said, "everyone is entitled to his own opinion, but not to his own facts."

America was founded to avoid tyranny of the majority. You can do whatever you want within the law as long as it doesn't hurt somebody else. Morons are entitled to be morons, but they are not entitled to force moronic rules on the rest of society.

And the rule of law is not restricted to Christians. Muslims are not allowed to kill nonbelievers, stone people who commit adultery, or cut the hands off of thieves. Mormons are not allowed to be polygamists. Seems fair to me.

?#@*&%!!

Chapter 28

Government Incompetence

The country is in the economic dumper. A relatively small group of people has caused the problem, and nobody has done anything about it. As a child, I believed that honesty, hard work, and playing by the rules would make a wonderful life. I don't suppose that was ever really true, but the illusion was there. School teachers taught it; my parents believed it, and so did most of the American people.

Somehow the Great Depression eased, our country was attacked, we fought the bad guys and won, and America went forward. The GI bill vastly increased the number of college-educated people. They found jobs and raised families, and everything was okay.

I believed that Congressmen and women were honest and smart, that the Federal Bureau of Investigation (FBI) was the best (they all had to be accountants or lawyers), the Food and Drug Administration (FDA) guaranteed our food and drug safety, business leaders were smart and had our interest at heart, and…well you get the idea.

DUMB!

The FBI can't even buy a computer system that works—neither can the Federal Aviation Administration. The FDA (the hierarchy at least) is incompetent, crooked, or too fearful of the repercussions from challenging big businesses and the political influence they wield. And don't get me started on the military/industrial complex. Can anyone justify star wars missile defense? Let's line up all of the senators that supported the bill. Give me a handful of BBs, and let me throw them at the senators. If they can catch all of them, let them build the system. Only a couple of missiles have to get through to end civilization.

When I was in the army in 1958, I lived in temporary barracks that were built in 1941 or thereabouts. We spent a lot of time cleaning and polishing these relics. One day the rule book said we had to clean the windows. First floor, no problem. Second floor, a small problem. To wash the windows, we had to climb out the window and stand on the sloping 1941 roof.

Mindful of the dangers to the young soldiers in their charge, the army required a safety belt while doing the job. The only problem was that there were no safety belts and nothing to hook up to on the barracks. Not to worry. Each of us scrubbers was issued two pieces of string to attach to our belts and also to something on the window frame. We lived. The rules were satisfied. And the rules were absolutely worthless.

It is not simply the military who plays this game. Congress wants food safety. It appoints a safety czar and, then being acutely sensitive to its fiscal responsibility, budgets for twenty-five inspectors to inspect the several hundred thousand sources of food around the world. On paper, we're protected. Except we aren't.

Our astronauts are protected. Probably the congressional dining rooms are. But our peanuts aren't. Our fish isn't. Our meat isn't. Our vegetables aren't. Lobbyists from the food industry probably would tell you how voluntary protections for the public are just good sense and good business, but they aren't. People die every day.

The "impossible" safety demands in the United States are routinely done in Japan, stuff like testing every cow for mad cow disease. Routine demands for perfection are met by purveyors of food. They build world-class cars and electronic stuff, too.

Why don't our regulators regulate what they're supposed to regulate? We shouldn't have to worry about mad cow disease. We should insist that the slaughterhouse test every animal. Downer cattle should not get into the food chain. If one does, the owner (or top corporate officer) should go to jail for five years. If a company imports any food product that's tainted, the owner (or top corporate officer) should go to jail for five years. If costs go up, costs go up.

Penalties must be applied to the top decision maker. If a ship sinks, it's the captain who is responsible. Line workers will do whatever is required or be fired. Corporate responsibility pays extremely well nowadays. We are entitled to get our money's worth.

It can be done. Other countries seem to have it figured out. In the United States, immediate profits seem to be more important than customer health. Constantly forcing suppliers to lower prices forces them to cut corners. For example, fouled waters in fish and shrimp farms are the responsibility of the U.S. buyers to know about. Sickening food products (particularly if people die) are akin to murder, and purveyors of the food are culpable. Ignorance of the law is no excuse when receiving a speeding ticket. There should be no escaping accountability for dangerous food products, no corporate shield for dodging responsibility for the purity of a food product.

Each day, when my sense of outrage wains a bit, I can count on the daily newspaper to revitalize my juices. Today's inspirational headline is "Administration Seeks to Restrict Antibiotics in Livestock." Now much has been said about nervous mothers pressing a pediatrician to prescribe an antibiotic for every minor malady their kids encounter. The theory is that when we all need antibiotics, the excessive inappropriate use will have taught the really mean bugs how to counter our last hope and kill us.

It's odd that the inappropriately named swine flu might

kill a lot of us because our pushy farmers are using antibiotics on healthy chickens, pigs, and cattle simply to encourage rapid growth. Before the haters put their pens to paper, I should say that I now own the family farm. The same honorable family has rented my land for more than thirty years, and I'm sure they carefully manage my part of our country's greatest natural resource.

The problem is the same one over and over again: corporations. When big business gets involved with anything, it wants profits now. However, that splendid insensitivity to the future lends itself to a few sleazy guys wrecking the financial industry, the airline industry, and just about every other major industry including the agriculture industry.

I don't think we will ever return farming to the days of horse-drawn plows and reapers, although a guy in Iowa tried it and actually made more money doing it. Thanks to the horses, he didn't have to spend any money on fertilizer or fuel and the horses produced a baby tractor every year.

I'm afraid the ideal farm is a thing of the past. Free-range chickens, pigs, and cows eating what God intended…and provides.

I suppose we've never been perfect. My uncle, who raised Hereford cattle as a profit-making hobby told stories of cancerous cattle being sold. He understood that the cancerous part would be cut away at the slaughter house; however, I don't remember seeing him eat a hamburger and he and my aunt always ordered steaks very well done.

Something must work. We aren't all dead. But it kinda makes you want to grow your own food and maybe become a vegetarian.

Then there is the drug problem. We supposedly test drugs carefully before approval, but we don't. It turns out that thousands of heart attack patients have been gobbling pills that bypassed FDA approval. We think nobody died.

I read that almost every type of drug we need, from aspirin to penicillin, is made outside of the United States. I can't think of a greater issue of corporate and governmental malfeasance. Are we crazy? We tolerate offshore corporate tax dodgers. We sacrifice American jobs to benefit corporate profits thanks to third-world desperation approaching slave labor. It's morally disgusting and inexcusable for a cheaper pair of jeans or a cheaper shirt. But at the very least, the health and welfare of the American people should be a horse of a different color.

Somehow it seemed different when the vendors were German or Swiss. (The myth of precision, fanatic cleanliness, and people like our ancestors in charge made it seem okay.) It may not be politically correct to say it, but India and China do not conjure up the same images; however, the blame really should be assigned to the greedy American corporations that enjoy the Indian and Asian hospitality and cut the purchase prices so low that their suppliers are forced to accept raw materials from hundreds of sources with less stringent requirements than the FDA would allow in the United States.

No doubt that is why prescription drugs are so reasonably priced and readily available to the sick and the needy. Wait a minute. They aren't reasonably priced. How can that be?

Not only could our homeland security be compromised and possibly jeopardized by incompetence or, God forbid, bio-terrorists, but also the saber rattling military in the United States and China would put a real crimp in our supply lines particularly if China were to become an enemy.

A clipping I saved said that George Orwell once remarked that "whether the British ruling class are wicked or merely stupid is one of the most difficult questions of our time, and at certain moments a very important question." It applies to our government as well.

?#@*&%!!

Chapter 29

Blue Double Cross

When I was a kid, doctors knew everything. They were valued members of every community. They knew their patients, and they knew their medicine. They made house calls. They fixed you up, and if necessary, they operated on you. They got paid in cash, a dozen eggs, a side of beef, or a new garage. It worked. But the new medicine was getting expensive so a bunch of doctors figured out a way to make it easier to pay for their services. They started Blue Cross/Blue Shield—the first paid doctors, the second paid hospitals or other medical services.

It was pretty slick. You paid a set monthly fee depending on the size of your family and maybe a few other facts the plan considered, and when you got sick, Blue Cross/Blue Shield paid 80% of the bills. No haggling, no restrictions, no second guessing by the home office. Doctors owned Blue Cross. Doctors were honest providers to be trusted. Pretty simple. No businessmen involved, no lawyers involved, no costly bureaucratic structures.

SOME THINGS REALLY WERE BETTER IN THE 1950s

I don't remember when health care started going bad, maybe with the compartmentalizing of the product. More research, more specialists, more pharmaceuticals, and more treatment options rendered a more complex billing environment that fostered a vastly enlarged billing structure and the pathway to a patient financial disaster.

Then there was company-provided health insurance. Operating on the theory that healthy workers made a healthy company bottom line, companies asked for a program, and insurance companies leapt at enlarging their core business.

You know what's coming don't you? Now, instead of a small Blue Cross office that verified your membership and wrote a check to the provider for 80% of your bill, we had a government-sized bureaucracy that thrived on nitpicking, delaying, and obfuscating until many people gave up and paid the small bills themselves. On larger bills, the ordeal of collecting the patient's due could include costly litigation and almost unendurable personal trials. I have not even mentioned the out-of-network scams that place the burden of proof on the frazzled patient or the family.

Having been a banker for a couple of years, I know that the float benefits of delay are a significant addition to the insurance companies' bottom line.

Single-pay, government-provided health insurance would come close to returning to the days of yesteryear.

Unfortunately, that probably won't solve everything. The *New York Times* printed a spate of assessments and grumblings by doctors and medical school professors about the need to fix or provide universal health care. The diminishing numbers of primary care doctors, Medicare payments favoring specialists, costly malpractice insurance, and whether the problems are a result of pure greed or the extremely burdensome medical school debts were discussed.

One thing not discussed was how the character defects of the brightest on Wall Street seem to have intruded on the nobility and personalities of aspiring physicians leading them to choose a calling that features high bucks, minimal patient contact, and, if they're really creative, regular office hours with no nights or weekends required. Oh, and nobody wants to practice in rural areas, dirt poor towns, or, the most neglected, Indian reservations.

There was always something truly American about becoming a physician. You work hard, endure privations, pay your dues, and strive for excellence, and suddenly the golden gates open. Fawning respect from merchants, a beautiful spouse, a big house, a country club, and several highly desired cars were expected. While the Yin is still there, the Yang of the empathetic, caring, house-call-making friend of the family is missing from the equation. Accountants and financial advisors have introduced cost-effectiveness, and lawyers have added malpractice, avoiding extra procedures and prohibiting any apologies or admissions of error that led to adversarial relationships rather than the former kindly concern of a learned friend.

Perhaps we should reconsider the phrase "practicing medicine." It tends to diminish the god-like rendering of the patient's needs after a thorough eight-minute consultation. If current standards suggest an immediate referral to a specialist, maybe we should concentrate on creating specialists. A popular anecdote about Albert Schweitzer has him saying that he could take an African native out of the jungle and teach him to do a respectable appendectomy after six weeks of training. A nurse practitioner gave me one of the most thorough physicals I have ever had. Perhaps we are spending too much on training doctors for situations they will never experience. Would anyone in a catastrophic auto accident prefer immediate treatment by a doctor over a navy corpsman just returned from Iraq?

?#@*&%!!

Chapter 30

Health Care

When you're old, health care is a tad more on your mind than it was when you were in your twenties. The health-care system isn't too bad if you're on Medicare, have a pension to supplement Medicare, or have the money to buy your own supplemental policy. However, for everyone under sixty-five who has a job without health-care benefits, or no job at all it is a fearful situation.

There is no reason for this problem to exist. The United States is the only major industrialized country in the world without universal health care. We spend more money per capita on health care than the other countries, and we rank woefully low on the world totem pole of healthy citizens. Why? Congressional corruption!

The highly touted, government-sponsored drug program is a textbook example of drug company lobbyists' total control of our legislators from both parties. Is there any other way to view the fact that Congress passed a law specifying our government is not allowed to negotiate lower prices for the mass purchase of any and all drugs? Bargaining with drug companies is not without precedent. It seems that the Veterans Administration has found a way to do this. A part of our government has demonstrated more sophisticated bargaining skills than our most esteemed politicians can muster.

The most interesting part of this situation is that the members of Congress wouldn't even have to waste their valuable fund-raising time to solve the health-care problem. A one-hour PBS special would show them just how it's done. Interviews with British, Swiss, German, and Japanese administrators would provide a fast track for legislative discussions.

And yes, there are minor flaws in each government's program, but none major enough that their citizens would give up this vital cushion. Republicans may challenge being forced to pay for some malingerers' coverage, but the thought of sitting at a ball game next to an untreated dangerously ill person cannot be attractive...even to them. And if angry recalcitrant Republicans think about it long enough, they'll realize that we are paying for them at exorbitant emergency room rates instead of the relatively modest costs of preventive care at a neighborhood clinic.

The University of Minnesota Health Service provided exemplary care fifty years ago for a minor stipend added to tuition.

I hope I haven't written anything too difficult for the people in Congress to understand. I'm not optimistic though.

I'm sure a bipartisan committee can find a reason not to help all of the Americans who employ them.

The Obama Administration has managed to pass the first significant health-care bill since Medicare. It took fighting every inch of the way, overcoming every nitpicking Republican ploy as well as the dealing with idiotic Tea Party anarchism in the streets, but it is done.

?#@*&%!!

Chapter 31

We're Not 9-1-1 for the World

With each passing day, there is another disaster somewhere in the world. President Obama delivers a supportive message of some sort and offers American aid to rescue, rebuild, and restore the injured or destitute to their former lives. In doing so, he echoes the traditional reaction of recent presidents.

Why? Former Congresswoman Pat Schroeder once said, "The United States cannot be 9-1-1 for the entire world." Perhaps in the era of the Marshall Plan following World War II, we had the capacity and the generosity to help the world's victims, but not now. We have our own victims that strain the ability of the government. The forgotten citizens of New Orleans come to mind, as do the homeless, and the 45 million Americans without health insurance.

We are throwing money away in Iraq to atone for the folly of our former pathetic leaders. Poor planning, worse execution, and endemic incompetence squandered billions of dollars for nothing. The only people who benefited from the

Iraq War were the bloated armaments industry and the contractors necessary to support our bedraggled military. Next time, we ought to simply hire some Hessians and keep the National Guard at home to look after our own needs.

Frankly I don't know what the hell we're doing in Germany, Korea, Japan, or anywhere else. It's a nice tour for the officers, but the Russians aren't massing tanks at the Fulda Gap, and the garrison in Korea would only delay the North Koreans for about a half an hour, and our economy could use those bucks we're handing to our allies.

And speaking of our allies, the *Wall Street Journal* published an analysis on December 4, 2009, complaining that our NATO partners were unwilling or unable to support us in the war in Afghanistan because most of them have little or no military capability left. The article damned the welfare-state mentality for the problem with a stunning judgment. "Welfare spending has crowded out defense spending. The political imperative of health care and pensions always trumps defense spending." What a novel idea—taking care of your own citizens rather than the military industrial complex. The final jab by the *Wall Street Journal* sort of shows where its bread is buttered. "The tragic irony of this year is that Democrats are rushing the U.S. down this same primrose entitlement path."

Whoa! I submit that it's about time for some entitlements. We ought to stop the foreign wars and foreign aid. America needs every dime it can get. Until every American city water system is new, every road is repaired, every dam is strengthened, every bridge is safe, every family is housed, every school is renewed, every person has health care, and we have a world-class passenger rail system, an up-to-date air traffic system, and fresh air to breathe, the world should be on its own.

Bring our troops home. Their families need them. We ought to be able to instruct the bad-acting countries in civilized behavior with the use of a couple of the bombs and missiles we've bought and paid dearly for over the last fifty years. No more soldiers or treasure needs to be wasted on the sorriest countries on the planet.

Ah, but what do we do about Iraq, Iran, Afghanistan, and al-Qaida? Let's use some of the weapons we already have. I suggest that we activate the missiles buried in the Dakotas. Unscrew the atomic warheads, replace them with good old TNT, and get to work. I hate to see our military people trashed in a never-ending attempt to civilize an uncivilized world. Nobody has been able to manage Afghanistan since the Romans ruled the world. However, these people respect power.

Why don't we simply tell them to stop making dangerous drugs for the world and stop trying to incite the Muslim world to kill us. Advise them to live peacefully or else we will send enough missiles to plow all of the soil in their part of Afghanistan and the part of Pakistan they control sufficiently so that whatever peaceful tribe moves in will have a head start on growing food or a suitable product for sale to the rest of the world.

Let's learn from history. Update gunboat diplomacy. If our problem is militant Muslims, have the majority of peaceful twentieth-first century Muslims clear up the problem. If they don't, simply use our paid-for and, hopefully, operational missiles to begin to erase the most likely Muslim-threatening locations and keep working up the chain until there are no more militants. They (functioning, modern Muslim governments) know who the militants are and where they are, and now it's time for them to eliminate the problem.

If this seems too extreme, why don't we simply cut off all of the benefits of the modern world from noncomplying Muslim governments. No financial ties, no transportation, no commercial ties of any kind—let them revert to living in the seventh century in the manner the militants seem to prefer. And the sooner we stop mortgaging our future to buy their high-priced oil, the better.

?#@*&%!!

Chapter 32

Some Things Never Change

When I was in college, still following my Republican heritage, there emerged a somewhat demented conservative hero named J. Bracken Lee who refused to pay his income taxes. Upset by the amount of American foreign aid at the time, he held back his tax money because he said "it was unconstitutional to use it to support a foreign power." He lost. I think he paid up rather than go to jail for his beliefs.

Being quick with a quip even then, I suggested that we should simply stop all foreign aid. People on the receiving end all seemed to resent or hate us anyway. Our Russian enemies would feel compelled to pick up the pieces and would quickly go broke, and that would solve another problem.

Conventional wisdom in the 1950s was to constantly enlarge our weapons systems. It seemed to be an appropriate move in our troubled world. And I am no stranger to weapons of mass destruction. I was nine when we dropped the atomic bombs on Japan. However, after the Russians got their bomb I don't remember ever being asked to duck and cover. I think even then our teachers knew that in case of an atomic war the more appropriate suggestion would be kiss your ass good-bye.

Nevertheless, I was aware of and believed in our weapons programs. Now I'd like to see these marvelous killing machines put to occasional use. Keep reading. I'm not advocating atomic war. It's just that we have this stuff. Because we have the capacity to end human life on the planet, what more do we need?

This is kind of a conundrum. It's hard to single out the people responsible for these things. At least some members of Congress are trying to put an end to ridiculous spending. They just voted down a bill to increase production of the F-22. As I understand it, this is the weapon we will likely use to challenge extraterrestrial invaders. That is, unless clever spies from our earthly enemies steal the plans and make an F-22+ of their own. The cost has increased exponentially since it was originally proposed in 1980, and not one F-22 has fired its weapons in anger...ever.

Are we crazy? Ill-equipped soldiers and marines are going into really mean battles with inadequate flak jackets, poorly thought out weapons carriers, and a host of other equally expensive mistakes. As I understand it, one of the better weapons we had in the Iraq wars was the planes affectionately known as the warthogs, and they've been around forever. And they were paid for.

According to what I read, the best thing going for the

F-22 is that it has "about 1,000 suppliers in forty-four states." Lobbyists for the F-22 are quick to point out that the workers required to produce these planes are voters. My personal feeling is that our money would be better spent on these same workers in all forty-four states if they were building roads, schools, bridges, and hospitals, or at the very least, on appropriate weapons for our troops to use in the wars we actually fight.

Think of the incredible waste that has taken place since World War II. Without wanting to sound too bellicose, I say let's check out a few of these babies and see how we do. We haven't had much success lately diplomatically. Maybe Teddy Roosevelt was right about talking softly and carrying a big stick. Let's take one of those missiles buried in the Dakotas, disarm the nuke, and drop one in the biggest park in Teheran. Then tell 'em we want to live in peace one way or another. While we're at it, how about one in Mogadishu's soccer stadium. We might be able to turn our stock buried in the Dakotas and actually accomplish something. Almost anything is better than destroying our military with ill-conceived adventures in places ungovernable for a thousand years.

I have no problem with anybody doing what they want with their country. I also realize that American hustlers have played and continue to play a big part in the corruption and exploitation of a large part of the developing world. But I haven't done anything, and neither have 99 44/100% of the American people.

?#@*&%!!

Chapter 33

Work, Workers, Bosses, and Owners

Fifty years ago, I took my humanities degree and went to work for a bank. As a trainee, I made $4,000 a year. The president of the bank (I heard) made $80,000 a year. He was my parents' age, worked hard, was smart, came up through the ranks, and earned it. I'm sure he enjoyed some additional perks and stock options, but that was okay. He was an honorable man, an honest man, and a man respected by his peers and his Board of Directors.

Bankers were different in those days. They paid attention to business. They followed the rules. Some were hard hearted, some were shysters, and some were outright crooks, but most did their best, looked after their customers, and were responsible, corporate citizens. I worked in the bond department. Ratings companies like Moody's and Standard & Poor's were respected and above reproach in their evaluations of investment options.

What in hell happened? Drugs? Rock 'n' roll? Casual dress? Greed?

When I bought a house twenty-three years ago, the mortgage guy wanted my W-2s, my wife's W-2s, my employment history, my credit history, and my blood type, and he probably got my fingerprints off the questionnaire. Now it seems like if you can sit or stand for thirty minutes and get mail, you're accepted. Then to up the ante (or the bank's pot), the bank bundles my loan with this fellow's loan and sell us to somebody else who bundles us with God knows how many others and dumps the package on another pigeon...who craps on the roof of the Federal Reserve System.

The president of my bank fifty years ago earned about twenty times my salary. Now the presidents of the big banks "earn" 315 times the salary of the worker bees, and their higher minions cut a similarly fat hog.

The way it works, they earn top dollar for creating these very profitable mortgage-backed derivatives that apparently looked great to other trusting, greedy investors. In reality, they were created out of air with little or no credible verification of value. The above-mentioned rating companies are now paid by the people they evaluate, not the buyers of their brains, integrity, and diligence who supported them in the past. Good ratings mean more business, bad ratings or (honest ratings) mean out of business.

Let's use the record business to explain derivatives. TIME LIFE puts out packages of the greatest hits of the 1970s. And they sell a lot of them because they buy the rights to the actual hits and the artists who made them famous. If today's banks were producing the CDs, they'd take a couple of big-name artists and throw them in with a bunch of cheesy cover groups and advertise them as the real thing. But it's not the real thing, and the mortgages were not of high quality, and the country is screwed!

And we have more reasons to thank the business world. We don't have to worry about robots taking over, they already have. Try to speak with a live operator when you call a company—any company—or a government, almost any government office except 9-1-1. Thank God for small favors.

I would really like to know the cost and benefits of turning public relations over to a machine. How much good will is sacrificed by putting customers, constituents, and the curious through the agony of trying to thread the corporate needle to reach the person who can actually help you? It's bad for business and politics. And the more "helpful" the machines get, the more frustrated the supplicant becomes. "To help us to serve you, please enter your twenty-digit account number followed by the pound key." I'm seventy-four years old. I touch type, and I play the piano, but I have real trouble entering twenty numbers on a cell phone, a roam phone, or my iPhone, and when I screw up, I have to start over or feign the inability to speak to get to a real honest-to-God live person.

I had to transact some major business with my bank, and

SOME THINGS REALLY WERE BETTER IN THE 1950s

nobody answered the phone. I suspect some corporate officer, after a long lunch with a telephone consultant returned to the home office with a figure that would head directly to the bottom line and that could be easily and instantaneously realized by firing every telephone operator at every branch in America. The phone system could handle it. Every extension had its own line with voicemail, piece of cake. Much moolah could be easily made.

Small problem. If you didn't know the name of the party you wanted or have a number to call, you were out of luck. And if you didn't leave a voicemail, you were shunted to a call center for help. At various times, I was "helped" by Shoreview, Minnesota; Sioux Falls, South Dakota; and Reno, Nevada (twice); only nobody could help me. As I begged to be given the secret number that would be answered, one of my helpers said he had been waiting for ten minutes for help on the secret number. I held on until I reached a banker I needed, but if I hadn't already been a customer and a stockholder, I would have been out of there in a matter of seconds.

I should say that the regional helpers were polite, sympathetic, and genuinely helpful, but they allowed that I was not the only disappointed customer they had encountered.

A news story about air travel reported that airline personnel are so upset by the state of their industry and working conditions that they don't seem to want to help troubled passengers anymore. They just don't care. Somebody in business had better realize that the entire customer base in every industry is waiting for somebody to recognize their value and really look after them.

I think businessmen were better when I was young. Captains of industry have probably never been known to ponder, "What would Jesus do?" in making management decisions; however, their concerns for self-protection usually provided an occasional benefit to ordinary workers and the community at large. When your workers live down the hill from your big house, your and your family's daily lives are exposed to anger and hostility if the little people feel ill-used. Fair treatment of your workers is just prudent management.

Even shielded by the corporate structure, the workers still know who you are and where you live. If, however, another corporation acquires your business, the entire balanced structure is dissolved, and with it the sense of community well being. Sometimes the new owners appreciate the productive environment and leave it untouched. More often, the dominant values of the new owners are simply productivity and profit. Local charitable contributions, tolerance of local traditions, and genuine concern for the community are discarded. Unfortunately, in today's world, concerns of reducing costs can mean closing a factory and shipping the means of production to Mexico.

This is frequently done by regular corporations. An even more vicious version of this process is a result of a leveraged buy-out of the parent corporation by a group whose intent is to strip and sell off all the pieces for a huge gain and simply shut the whole thing down—with no thought for the workers, the communities, and the pension obligations. And it's all perfectly legal.

I am reminded of an old saying, "God sees everything and waits." I hope so.

?#@*&%!!

Chapter 34

Making More Morons

In a world that desperately needs clean power, better food production and distribution, universal health care, and a host of other noble solutions to the problems of mankind, we have managed to channel the talents of computer programmers and greedy business people into a malevolent mix that threatens the quality of life in the United States (and possibly the world as it catches up).

We are producing big-eyed, big-fingered lumps of children. A slight modification of the society predicted when television assumed its role as babysitter, and perhaps more insidious since TV programs usually change hourly and video games go on forever until carpal tendon problems or exhaustion takes over the body.

The specter of a generation of useless slugs would be bad enough. But the vulgarity and brutality of the most popular games and the glorification of lawlessness and violent death suggest that it's time to push parental duties beyond shopping with their children and asking if they've done their homework.

?#@*&%!!

Chapter 35

Older People Could Use a Little Help

I haven't had many interruptions while gathering my thoughts for this book, but my telephone rings with uncommon frequency. My phone calls usually involve business, friends, situations where immediacy is involved (vehicle failure, broken necessities, a loved one in need), and things I am interested in.

Unfortunately, my phone calls rarely meet my requirements. It may be the ugly side of technology simply rearing its head again (they call because they can), criminal (preying on the elderly to rob them), or just another example of our technological nightmares (automated recorded calls spit out by the millions).

Apparently, this does not trouble the thirty-year-old bureaucrats charged with the well-being of our communication system. A phone call to my age group requires an answer, even when it involves prying our elderly bodies out of a chair and hobbling across the room. I submit that this can be a trying process for the infirm only to be harangued by a recorded breathless pitch for a worthless car warranty, a scam trip to Florida (including a cruise and several glorious days at a marginal motel), or spending my declining days in a long-term care facility.

Offers to remove my name from their lists have proved to be ineffective or worse because I have received a half dozen more calls from the same outfit after my request.

Am I to understand that current technology cannot catch these irritating and dangerous solicitors? Am I to understand that this is really of no concern to the regulators we pay or to the Congressmen and women we pay? How can they permit a few business creeps (I'm being kind) to irritate and possibly endanger our elderly? More importantly, what do they intend to do about the criminal element who seem to be immune to supervision, regulation, or incarceration?

And it isn't just the phones. Where are the postal inspectors? How is it possible that they fail to notice the thousands (millions?) of bogus contest solicitations that require only $7.75 to confirm your status as a winner? How about the strong suggestion that a small purchase will almost guarantee a new car as your prize? Do any of our highly paid postmasters wonder why a P.O. box in Las Vegas receives millions of envelopes addressed by faltering hands?

How about the banks that process the thousands of checks written by these same faltering hands? Do they ever meet and evaluate the owners of these scamming accounts? A recent *Wall Street Journal* article said that even after a family member with power of attorney had virtually shut down a parent's account, the bank kept honoring these criminal checks and slapped multiple overdraft fees on the account. What is going on?

?#@*&%!!

Chapter 36

Illegal Drugs

My maternal grandparents didn't drink booze in any form. As far as I know, my mother never drank liquor until prohibition. Suddenly, the forbidden fruit gained appeal. In later life, I rarely saw my mother take a drink. My father made up for her and was probably a functional alcoholic. He never missed work, but things were a bit blurred after five o'clock.

A social worker speaking to a gathering of anxious prep school parents said that about 10% of all drinkers abuse the product. The ratio for marijuana smokers is approximately the same. Luckily for society, 90% of us are able to enjoy these pleasures without surrendering to them. Actually pot seems to be considerably better for the body than alcohol.

This does not mean that all illegal drugs qualify as manageable. Heroin, cocaine, and the like are not harmless. And the most insidious high is methamphetamine. It's cheap, readily available, very addictive, and deadly.

Pot, in my limited middle-aged experience, was a wonderful enhancement of appreciation for almost everything and never produced a hangover. The social worker did allow that 10% of the kids (or adults) who try pot can disappear into a hazy, unproductive life, but in my limited sphere of observation, no pothead ever started a fight or a riot or tried to tear a bar apart. In fact, a famous folk singer sang about the most raucous act of a stoned person was when he tried to break into a candy machine to satisfy the munchies.

The drug problem is out of control. The "just say no" campaign does not work, and, just as in prohibition, the criminal providers have nearly torn the country apart. More and more drug-fighting professionals are speaking out in favor of decriminalizing the personal use of marijuana. Legalizing (and taxing) the sale of marijuana would presumably ensure a safe, standardized product and restrict the sale to those of legal age. And removing the enormous revenues from the criminal distribution operations might help police by freeing up officers to concentrate on the deadlier drugs.

It would also be helpful to classify addictions as illnesses rather than criminal acts and free up space in our prisons for truly dangerous offenders.

I should state here that I haven't smoked a joint for over thirty years and probably consumed less than three dime bags in my lifetime. However, I liked it. And if it were legal, I'm afraid nightly martinis would be a thing of the past.

?#@*&%!!

Chapter 37

Punishment Needs Some New Standards

How can you deny communion to a Catholic politician who espouses or merely recognizes abortion as a personal decision when you allow known pedophile priests to give and take communion for twenty or thirty years?

How can you immediately jail a kid for stealing $100 from a 7-Eleven and allow house arrest in a $7 million apartment for an admitted felon who stole $50 billion? How can you have white-collar prisons with limited security, tennis courts, and woodworking jobs (making furniture for high-ranking government officials) for major economic criminals who have brought ruin to thousands of families and caused illnesses and suicides?

Do college educated, wealthy crooks need to be protected from the traumas of a brutal prison environment? If so, why? List your reasons.

Personally, I feel that spending a few years with a lascivious 300-pound cellmate might be the best deterrent available in today's justice system.

?#@*&%!!

Chapter 38

The Immigration Problem

Change is hard. America has almost always welcomed immigrants in one way or another. Unfortunately, often it was as cheap laborers. In most cases, the new arrivals were exploited until they learned the language and the ways of the new world. As they prospered, they became acceptable, absorbed, and a valued part of the community.

The key element was learning English. In almost every case, children led the way. Lately, large numbers of immigrants have established colonies that are impervious to the need for English as a part of daily life in America. Obvious examples include Hispanic Miami and Los Angeles and Chinatowns in some major cities and other insular foreign enclaves.

Throughout our history, people have revered their cultural heritage, but in a diminished role because they were first and foremost Americans.

New arrivals have to live by America's rules. An Islamic woman can cover her head, but not her face if she wants a driver's license or passport. Requiring special facilities for washing before praying or practicing religious laws that are contrary to U.S. laws is inappropriate. This is understandable. People visiting Muslim nations are unable to drink alcohol (at least in public) and are subjected to other laws of the land.

Welcome to all who want to become Americans. Just don't come here and expect to do as you please while taking advantage of our unique opportunities. And for sure, don't come here to screw with us!

?#@*&%!!

Chapter 39

What We Don't Know Can Hurt Us

Air travel is starting to become scary. As usual, the Federal Aviation Administration has opted for study as opposed to making and enforcing the tough rules it is charged to provide to protect the traveling public.

It seems that the dual role of promoting the aviation business and ensuring the safety of airline passengers is skewed in favor of the industry. Scant inspection of the outsourcing of airplane repairs in foreign countries, the tolerance of flying airplanes on intercontinental routes with potential catastrophic mechanical hazards uncorrected, and the frighteningly slow requirements of correcting known flaws on scheduled airlines should be enough for some raised congressional eyelids, but it gets worse.

There is almost no oversight of the growing use of feeder airlines. These are planes operated by relatively unknown airline companies that deliver small-town passengers to the major airline hubs. They display the insignias and designs of the larger airlines they service, are booked as if they are subsidiaries of the major airlines, and supposedly provide the level of skills and safety of the large airline. Not so! Seven out of the last eight airline crashes have involved feeder airlines.

In fact, it's hard to catalog the frightening inadequacies this situation presents. First there's experience. Major airlines require more than 4,000 hours of experience for a pilot to be hired. Feeders will take pilots with as few as 250 hours of flying experience. And that's usually in smaller, slower, and older piston-powered planes. Major airlines fly long routes with minimum pilot involvement except for avoiding turbulence, slight route or altitude adjustments, and remaining alert to possible catastrophic events. Often, the copilot takes off and the pilot lands the plane, and that's it (allowing for the considerable anxiety caused by crowded airports and bad weather).

The novice pilots make many takeoffs and landings at large and small airports (without radar, a control tower, or sophisticated navigational aids). With often just one runway to use, weather (cross winds, rain, fog, snow, and sleet) requires a lot of skills and experience to survive. This is a lot to ask from a pilot with 250 hours of experience, often gathered in warm climates and favorable weather where many of the training schools are located. Coping with bad weather can be a daunting task even for experienced, major-airline pilots. A major airline's plane crashed in Washington, D.C., years ago because the pilot, used to flying mostly in the south, failed to de-ice the wings before taking off.

Add to the situation low pay, brutal schedules, and little or no supervision of adherence to the rules for feeder pilots. Many pilots live as cheaply as possible, often far from their flight base, and consequently arrive at the job without sleep (after catching a free ride overnight with a sympathetic airline).

What to do? Nothing. No matter what the safety boards, the crash investigators, and the public interest groups say, the Federal Aviation Administration seems more inclined to maintain the status quo than to take a firm stand to protect the flying public.

?#@*&%!!

Chapter 40

Guns

I own a couple of guns. One is a double-barreled shotgun (410) last fired in the 1950s. The other is a hand gun I purchased a few years ago (a .38 revolver to protect my family from possible crazies who might invade our home). I understand pheasant and duck hunters. I don't care for either bird as food (having been forced to eat them during WWII and biting into a pellet my mom and dad missed).

I enjoyed firing an M-l during basic training and later a .45 pistol and a Grease (machine) gun during summer camp in the Army Reserve. But I never felt the need for an AK-47, an Uzi, or any other military weapon, or, for that matter, the need to shoot Bambi. There is a .50 caliber weapon capable of disabling a tank that is particularly popular at the Arizona gun shops that are arming the Mexican drug dealers. Are we insane?

Normal law-abiding hunters and trap shooters don't need military weapons!

I have two fantasies. One is assembling a panel of clergy from all of the major religious communities and having each member of Congress explain his or her support for the gun lobbies that pay for their legislative skills. The other is to have a platoon of U.S. Marines demonstrate the "legal" fire power available in this country by hosing down the National Rifle Association office building and the homes of the officers and board of directors.

Why do we allow this?

How many people in America earn a living from weapons? Maybe 100,000 workers at Smith & Wesson, Remington, Reuger, and Colt. Let's double it to be safe. Say 200,000 people work for all of the gun manufacturers in the country. How about licensed gun dealers? 50,000? Unlicensed dealers? 200,000? Being charitable, a half million people are capable of terrorizing 300 million law-abiding citizens...for money! Are we insane?

Because we have an active military-industrial complex, we can figure that the honest arms industry would still exist to make weapons for our fighting men, shotguns and rifles for sportsmen, and handguns for police officers and worried citizens who pass a background check to protect their families. So most of the legitimate jobs will still exist.

All we have to do is weed out the guys who import AK-47s, Uzis, and Mac-10s and pedal them everywhere to gangs, drug dealers, and crazies. Then stop the promoters from renting the local legion hall or some state-owned facility and handing out guns to the crazies with enough bucks to arm themselves.

I know there are laws to prevent idiot parents from leaving loaded guns where young children can find them. How about a law to prevent unlicensed gun dealers from arming these morons with a bad attitude who open fire on schools, family reunions, or post offices?

?#@*&%!!

Chapter 41

Israel

Why don't the Jews just buy a slice of Baja, California, or a part of the Dominican Republic and declare it Israel? Aipac can afford it. It's not without precedent. Theodor Herzl, the founder of the Zionist movement, was in favor of accepting the fertile "white highlands" of British East Africa (now Uganda) for a safe, uncontested Jewish "homeland" when it was offered by Prime Minister Arthur Balfour in 1902.

According to the Balfour Declaration, Great Britain waited until 1917 to propose that "Palestine be reconstituted as the National Home of the Jewish people." The war cabinet tried to accommodate everyone involved in the war effort by stating "that nothing shall be done which may prejudice the civil and religious rights of existing non-Jewish communities in Palestine."

The traditional Palestine (formerly administered by the British government) is the symbolic home of three great religions. Arab Palestinians' historic claim on the territory currently occupied by Israel is clearly the equal of the Jews' claim. Israel won several wars and expanded its portion of Palestine awarded to it at the termination of the British mandate. And as of now, Israel is militarily superior to the various Arab/Palestinian/insurgent armies.

If these disputes were tribal problems in Africa or Banana Republic border difficulties, Americans would be less troubled (to our shame). But because Palestine is a cause celebre for the entire militant Muslim world, it currently dominates nearly every discussion of world peace, diplomatic relations, and world trade. Israel's establishment of permanent settlements in disputed lands and heavy-handed treatment of Palestinians living in these lands constantly exacerbates an extremely tense situation. Because of past U.S. involvement with Israel, we are subjected to the hostile reactions of the militant Muslim throughout the world, particularly in Afghanistan, Iraq, and Iran.

Even without the threat of a nuclear exchange, the future security of Israel and its people is not what most loving parents and grandparents would wish for their families. Using the United States as an example, most Jewish families do not elect to maintain a bunker mentality and continue to live in changing neighborhoods that feature crack dealers and hookers on every corner and where the threats of robbery, assault, and mayhem are the order of the day. It is just a matter of time before accurate rockets can reach everywhere in Israel, not to mention local suicide bombers.

I suggest that Jews are no less holy or out of touch with God as a result of living in the United States, France, or Spain. There is no logical reason to turn an entire country into Masada or continue to inflame the whole world. If we can take the London Bridge to Lake Havasu, Arizona, someone can take the Wailing Wall to Baja, California, or any other safe, hospitable country. And think what a garden spot the Israelis could create with what they save on weapons.

?#@*&%!!

Chapter 42

Blacks

This is a hard one. I grew up in South Dakota in the 1940s. There were no blacks in my town. Amos & Andy was one of my favorite radio programs. I didn't know they were black. One was dumb (Andy), one was smart and nice (Amos), and one was a crook (Kingfish). From my perspective, the program was a very funny presentation of the human condition. I never cared for the TV show. I never realized the perceived damage in the black community that the program represented, although that may be why I didn't care for it.

I'm a professional musician, a pianist. My favorite jazz pianists were black. My lifelong wish was to attain a smidgeon of the skills that made Errol Garner, Oscar Peterson, and Gene Harris so enjoyable.

When I booked entertainers, black artists were patient with the shortcomings of almost every performing site and polite in their dealings with me. Particular standouts were the Fifth Dimension and Bill Cosby.

I begin with these thoughts because I have never had a personal grievance or reason to judge blacks harshly as a group; however, as an ethnic group, blacks are in big trouble.

I blame the elimination of railroad passenger service for the demise of the black family structure. From the late 1800s to 1969, railroad Pullman porters contributed mightily to the structure and financial well being of black communities. Per a *New York Times* article published on April 4, 2009, on a Pullman porters tribute, by Jennifer 8. Lee, "the job of porter was considered for decades one of two good jobs for black men in the United States. (The other was working in the post office.)"

These men had families, owned homes, disciplined their children, and inspired them to achieve successful adult lives. According to Larry Tye, author of *Rising From the Rails*, porters "are—to a disproportionate extent—the fathers, grandfathers and uncles of the black professional class today." And these "men have retained certain dignity (at eighty to one-hundred years of age). When we find them they are dapper. They are men even at this age, who wear suits and ties."

In an age of single multiple mothers, drug use, and poverty, the only role models in the neighborhood are the pimps, drug dealers, and the highly paid professional athletes on TV. This must change. When black kids enjoy and do well in school, they are derided as trying to "act white." All kids are as smart as they are expected to be. This may be why parochial schools and good charter schools produce smart,

SOME THINGS REALLY WERE BETTER IN THE 1950s

achieving graduates. A respected black writer said that he had a real bear of a teacher who simply wouldn't let him fail. "He didn't care that I was poor or black or troubled at home, he said, math is an exacting discipline. There is only one right answer. Get it or get out."

Bill Cosby is encouraging black men to stop fathering children they don't intend to raise or support. If something doesn't change soon, the black community and the country as a whole are going to be in deep trouble.

This abdication of adult guidance seems to be a recent development. An article in the *New York Times* exploring Supreme Court nominee Sotomayor's childhood listed examples of her recollections of growing up poor in the projects with an intact family. All of the fathers were employed. Families had dinner together every night. Going to school was considered important. Positive attitudes were key. "Where you are is not who you are. We lived in a place where some people thought there was limited opportunity. We never thought that." Another key element to childhood growth is that at that time, "parents were never visible but always present. They had eyeballs in the building."

I don't know what the answer is to this problem. Early childhood education? Removal of young children to boarding schools? Providing some sort of structured, normal life with caring adults, friends, and inspirational teachers supported by a healthy diet and lifestyle? I suppose there are those who would decry the costs involved, but compared to a future of criminal mayhem and the unbelievable costs of our prison system, preventive action would be the least costly solution. Not to mention the incalculable benefits the kids might give back to the community as responsible adults.

?#@*&%!!

Chapter 43

Dying

Dying isn't something to dwell upon, but when you're in your seventies, the subject pops up more frequently than it used to. I subscribe to a lot of magazines. The youth-oriented ones occasionally pay tribute to us geezers by advising their principle demographic group what to avoid lest you should look like your dad.

Almost every business magazine concentrates on how to avoid outliving your resources, when and how to pass on any excess to your children, or how to continue to care for them from the grave. All good stuff to know, but when they begin to discuss long-term care options, they leave out a critical factor—how to get out before life becomes really unpleasant.

My 102-year-old aunt died after spending nearly ten years in a nursing home. My mother died nearly twenty years ago from a heart attack. It was a shock, but it was mercifully quick and understandable. My father died while I was in college (also from a heart attack)—a shock, but something that just happened. Other family members died, but I hadn't been there at the time.

With my aunt, as the only remaining elderly blood relative, I played a bigger role in her life. When her house became too much to handle, my wife and I helped her get rid of her excess and move into an apartment in an assisted living building. Later, after numerous hospitalizations, we helped her move into a more assisted living facility (small apartment, no kitchen stove to cause problems) and finally, after one more hospitalization, into a nursing home.

My aunt appreciated the cleanliness of the facility, the kindness of the staff, even the food. She could still see, hear, and talk. Visiting her (I lived three hundred miles away) was not unpleasant. We talked and ate together in a private dining room, and I took care of her needs—new clothing, business, etc. I felt that she was as happy as her deteriorating condition would allow.

Then gradually her body began to give out. Her hearing got worse with every visit. We could still communicate, but I began to write questions we were discussing. That worked. She read the paper daily, even with macular degeneration, until her sight simply got too bad. Then her roommate died. She had others, but never really connected with them. Finally, small strokes limited her speech to the extent that I couldn't understand what she said. While I believe her mind remained intact, she was essentially cut off from the world.

She would respond to simple staff questions (usually

shouted directly into her better ear) about more food or comfort issues, but I found it impossible to talk with her. I tried to mitigate the situation by nodding, saying "I think so," or appearing to understand and agree with her statements, while hoping that I hadn't agreed to participate in a violent act or to spirit her away to a new apartment or something. I really felt uneasy in these discussions so mostly I just held her hand.

Before, while she could still talk normally, she had often said, "your mother and father were the lucky ones." During the ten years I visited her, I was struck by the numbers of inventoried elderly, sitting head down in wheelchairs, parked in front of large TV sets, or in hallways, waiting with or without their "buttons" to die.

It's unbelievably sad. It would certainly be better for them and society if we simply gathered the family to say good-bye and gave the elderly (and everyone like them in the country) a pill or a shot that would release them from a life that really isn't a life.

?#@*&%!!

Chapter 44

Summing Up

I haven't mentioned my high school teacher's suggestions yet. His first suggestion was to tell more about myself at the beginning of the book, which I did. His second suggestion was to deal with a subject only once. I tended to spew it out as each irritant surfaced not necessarily in a coherent order. I have followed this suggestion. His third suggestion was to save the most important stuff for last. I hope I succeeded. And his final suggestion was to offer a little hope for the future.

When you're old, you're inclined to think you're still young in spirit. A lot of people purport to feel this way. I'm not so sure about them, but I think I know why I am.

My first job was at a giant bank where I observed colleagues thirty years older than I slowly advance toward the corner office ten yards back of me doing the same thing I was doing. You could watch the life drain out of them as their hair added new shades of gray. I left.

Next, I worked as a traveling salesman for a giant corporation. It was a good company, the travel was okay, the products were wonderful, but the job was not exciting. And that pretty much is the kiss of death. Add to it a marital breakup in a strange state, and that ended it.

Back home, after a brief stint as a jack-of-all-trades in a small ad agency, I was offered a chance to join a booking agency that sold pop concerts to colleges in seven Midwest states, and it turned out to be wonderful. Dealing with college kids and their student activities people was great fun. Spartan travel conditions didn't bother me. Late-night post-concert wrap-ups were fun, and I met a large number of future famous artists when they were starting out. Most were still gracious, grateful for any kind of help, and gave inspired performances with the hope of achieving great success soon. Our agency also developed local acts and booked them in mini-concerts that were economical noon-hour diversions for community colleges as well as major universities. The job lasted eight years, and it was wonderful.

Drawing on my earlier ad agency experiences, I began to write radio ads as a freelancer. Freelancing is iffy when you're starting out, and when I became increasingly involved with a major electronics retailer, they offered me a full-time job and I took it. I wrote newspaper ads and radio ads. I wrote what I thought was funny stuff; the president (my boss), who was my age, laughed, and that's all it took. Oh, and the ads worked. We were mobbed, and we sold a lot of stuff.

My final salaried ad writing was done for the biggest electronics company in America: Best Buy. The company was much smaller then, but I contributed to its growth. Everyone in the ad department was twenty years younger than I, including the bosses. Their ideas gave me a youthful perspective, their fun kept me young, and their enthusiasm was catching. I didn't think about it in my daily life, but when I spent time with my classmates or other people my age, I noticed that in most of them the peppiness of youth had already been washed away by adulthood.

I eventually left Best Buy (fired by my young boss). I still identified with my young colleagues, but my young boss was beginning to have his own youth washed away by adulthood and importance. It was time to go anyway.

Now, as for my hopes for the future. America needs more of the same thing it has always had, a new crop of young people—eager kids, diverse, confident, and maybe leavened enough by the tough economic times to grow up sooner and strive for something better, something creative, something of genuine value to society. To accomplish this, we need more teachers like I had in high school—teachers who are able to inspire as well as impart the necessary core knowledge to students. Education is not a party or a video game or a gadget that does everything for you. It's a collection of disciplines and skills that open the doors of the world even when the batteries run down. Right now the world appears to be coming apart at the seams, and it may if we continue to amuse ourselves and forget that life requires a lot of work. Parents have to raise healthy children with good values by providing good homes and demonstrating good habits. And no matter what they may say, kids want a structure in which to develop and a caring, protective home.

As for me, I've been lucky enough to keep thinking young, keep pleasing people of all ages with my dance band, and continue to maintain awareness of what's going on in contemporary society. It's certainly interesting, but when you consider everything going on today, things really were better back then.

Epilogue

You know by now about how wonderful the good old days were. I'm sure that part of it was that my body was younger then. You don't read many books about how wonderful the good old bodies are. Lyric poets don't extol the virtues of blurry eyesight, failing hearing, disappearing hair where you want it, and growing hair where you don't. There are no paeans for aches. The songs are all about blue skies, not gray skies.

Nobody said it was going to be easy. Few among us reach three score and ten years of age without needing a surgeon, a handful of pills, or a trained ear for counsel. The days of sliding into home at the family picnic are gone forever. Walking replaces running. Scatter rugs have become a threat. Comfort vies with a possibly rewarding new experience. It's too bad TV programs today pale in comparison with TV programs of yesterday. Luckily, music brings back the old zing by refreshing our memories.

Remember, it ain't over until the fat lady sings. There are still wonderful books to read, trips to take, foods to taste, animals to love, and someone to share your life with (if you're lucky). New experiences can restore a youthful vigor to your life. Attitudes are as important as ever. As long as you have your health and the strength to do it, participate. Just do it!

About the Author

Lou Johnson is retired and living in Tucson, Arizona. He still feels capable of writing pithy advertising copy, playing the piano, and speaking in public. He has opinions about almost everything and is willing to share them. He and his wife loved living in Minnesota, but prefer to spend their declining years in an ice-free zone.